# Revelation

# Explained

# REVELATION EXPLAINED

*The Light of Prophecy Shines Bright*

By

## K.J. SOZE

Niagara Falls, NY

# Copyrights

# Contents

# Introduction

uckle your seatbelts and move your tray tables into their upright, locked position. We're preparing for takeoff into the cloudy skies of end-time prophecies, picking up where my first book, The Message for the Last Days, left off. Readers who are not experienced with the adverse conditions of Revelation would do best to start there, because the three hundred pages of background and analysis are crucial for understanding what follows here. While it may be tempting to fly towards the sunset, there are no shortcuts in Bible prophecy.

While you will find references to previous chapters from The Message for the Last Days, it is not imperative that you revisit them. This book will summarize their key points. The references to previous chapters are for those who want to research further if the summaries do not provide enough information. Please do not be concerned that this book starts with Chapter 17. Just be aware that this is not a starter course about Revelation or Bible prophecy.

Revelation Explained works under the premise that the reader already knows the basics about Bible prophecy and is ready to learn more. There are two other established bases that are fundamental to know before advancing into deeper levels of prophecy. These are extremely important:

## Key Starting Points

**Interpretation** – The Bible interprets itself in most cases of prophecy, with repeated passages from the Old Testament to the New. We do not personally interpret the Bible, as there is no subjective meaning within private interpretation (see Appendix 1). Interpretation is "revealed" by the Holy Spirit.

**Language** – We are far removed from the original language and cultures that wrote inspired words from the Holy Spirit. We often rely on translators to place modern wording into ancient biblical context. This approach does not always succeed, and translators have bias. However, since the Bible interprets itself within its own context and we have commentaries from the apostles, we can understand what prophecy is about. We also have the benefit of the Greek language quoting Hebrew and Aramaic, so we should feel confident about what the future holds.

Complex topics such as end timing found in the books of Daniel and Revelation cannot be understood without a foundation. Please review this summary of my previous book before diving into the deep end of Bible prophecy.

The Message for the Last Days will help you understand the framework needed for such topics as the Day of the Lord, the Mark of the Beast, and the Great Tribulation Period.

## Summary of The Message for the Last Days

**Interpretation Principles** – This is the first step in understanding the Bible. This section explains how we often "translate" the Bible to fit our preconceived notions, or how we let the Bible speak for itself. Do we use subjective or objective interpretation methods? How do we deal with figurative language found within Bible prophecies? See Chapter 1 – Bible Interpretation Principles and Appendix 1.

**The Land Promise and Covenants** – Why did God create the earth and us? Find out in chapters 2 through 5 of The Message for the Last Days. The covenants God made with His people over time are vital to understand. This background helps us learn about the Kingdom of Heaven and future plans yet to be revealed about heaven and earth.

**The Second Coming of Christ** – Is there a rapture before the second coming of Christ, or is the rapture and second coming the same event? The reason God is coming to dwell on earth is revealed in light of the land promise to Abraham and repeated references in the New Testament. See Chapter 6.

**The Resurrection of the Dead** – The apostle Paul stated this is the cornerstone of the Christian faith in 1 Corinthians 15:12-19. Without the resurrection, there is no Christianity. Was he speaking of a bodily resurrection, in spiritual terms, or both? Chapters 7-9 explain our current position of a new life in Christ while differentiating from life after death.

**Judgment Day** – Find out about the paradox of God's judgment in chapters 10-15. Does judgment happen quickly, or does it take "1000" years for Christ to judge the entire Earth? Before comprehending the rationale of His judgment, we need to behold God's nature compared to human nature, along with knowing God's will compared to free will.

When we read the Bible as a vehicle for prophecy related to the end times, three key events take on outsized importance. The second coming, the resurrection of the dead and judgment stand out as significant focal points. Events before and after this cluster are of great interest that deal with the tribulation period and the millennial kingdom. However, these three events are so well documented and repeated that we must use them as markers to help us understand less clear passages about tribulation, the antichrist, or God's wrath.

So how might one refer to the theories found within these pages? For labeling purposes and ease of reference, we can call it a futurist view contrary to post-millennialism, preterism, or views that refer to the Kingdom of Heaven as fully established in the past. The Kingdom of Heaven and salvation are ongoing since Christ walked the earth during His first advent. See salvation in past, present, and future terms while noticing verb tense usage of passages found in Appendix 2. The language of the Bible itself serves to identify a work-in-progress method while comparing Christ's completed works to future works yet to be completed.

This book will distinguish Christ's reign at the present time (in the unseen realm) to His future reign in the physical realm. Passages about a future physical reign on earth use root words that are not meant to be spiritualized using figurative language.

A future reign of Christ on earth can be considered to fulfill all remaining prophecies that have not been realized. We'll examine how the word of God, through hundreds of passages from the Old Testament, create the plausible premise for Christ's future kingdom within Revelation as the culmination of the promises dating back to the Garden of Eden on down through to the New Testament times.

Knowing this material helps deepen our faith. A better comprehension of prophecy allows constructive and time-sensitive conversations with people in our spheres of influence, especially in relation to current events. You do not need to be a Bible scholar to have these discussions. There is no need to have debates about complex topics such as Ezekiel's visions, Daniel's 70 weeks, or how the Mark of the Beast will be rolled out. Once we see the signs unfold, we will be prepared to help those around us as life becomes more difficult in the coming days.

A word of warning – if you are looking to find out what the Mark of the Beast is without understanding what righteousness and wisdom are (and how they are related to each other), you will be disappointed. Only the wise and righteous will understand end times, recognize the signs, and avoid the wrath of judgment as warned by the Creator who expects us to know His plans in advance.

> **Daniel 12:8-10** *I [Daniel] heard, but I did not understand. Then I said, "O my lord, what shall be the outcome of these things?" He [the Messenger] said, "Go your way, Daniel, for the words are shut up and sealed until the time of the end. Many shall purify themselves and make themselves white and be refined, but the wicked shall act wickedly. And none of the wicked shall understand, but **those who are wise shall understand**.*

*2 Thessalonians 2:9-12* *The coming of the lawless one is by the activity of Satan with all power and false signs and wonders, and with all wicked deception for those who are perishing, because they refused to love the truth and so be saved. Therefore, God sends them a strong delusion, so that they may believe what is false, in order that all may be condemned who did not believe the truth but had pleasure in unrighteousness.*

**Note from the author** – please remember to write a review or leave a rating to help spread the Word after reading this book. There is new information in this book that has not been shared before. You can visit Goodreads or my website for more information. Thank you and God Bless. KJ

# Chapter 17

## *What Is the Timeline for the Last Days?*

Perhaps there has never been a book so misunderstood and so misinterpreted as the Apocalypse (Revelation), written by John, an apostle of Christ. Despite the development of numerous charts issued in attempts to map out the seven bowls, seven trumpets, and seven seals compared to the Day of the Lord, Great Tribulation Period, and Judgement Day, Biblical theoreticians and scholars have struggled to fully map out the correct sequence of events. Rather than concern ourselves with what others have suggested, since the views are many, we'll instead use the language of these prophecies to devise an inclusive timeline chart based upon the original Data.

Tracing the origin of prophecy stands as the best method to learn how prophecies build upon each other until we reach the last visions received by John. We will start with an example concept from the first and last chapters of Revelation.

Revelation 1:1a *"The revelation of Jesus Christ, which God gave him to show to his servants the things that must **soon** take place."*

Revelation 22:20 *"He who testifies to these things says, 'Surely I am **coming soon**.' Amen. Come, Lord Jesus!"*

It is difficult to avoid getting caught in the brambles of seemingly contradictory phrases and confusing statements related to the concept of timing. How could Christ have stated that He "is coming soon" when He spoke these words thousands of years ago? Did He already come spiritually into our lives? Did He mean He would physically come again to earth sooner, rather than later? We will find that "soon" often means "swift or quick" as derived from Ezekiel and others shown below.

The apostles thought Christ would establish His kingdom physically on the earth (Acts 1:6-7). They knew His heavenly kingdom was established already and permanent, but they also knew about prophecies yet unfulfilled wherein Christ would literally sit on His earthly throne. All throughout the New Testament (N.T.) we see hope of a future, physical, second coming.

9

# What Does "No More Delay!" Mean?

Christ's "delay" from a human perspective has led to an outcropping of beliefs that interpret Christ's kingdom as spiritual or heavenly based, not including an earthly base in the future. For the impatient, passages that speak of a kingdom on earth are sometimes interpreted as fulfilled by the Church on earth in a spiritual sense. These theories are the equivalent of snatching low-hanging fruit and demonstrate a willingness to settle that is not completely supported by the prophecies.

By trying to assert that these prophecies have already come to pass, people have often watered down the core concepts found in prophecy and transferred these passages into non-physical realm meanings. These interpretations fit with ancient Greek and earlier beliefs that state the physical realm is corrupt, or neutral at best, while only the spiritual realm is good. In these cases, we see prophecies of believers getting transported to Heaven, then the earth blows up in the end. This is a concept that some prominent Greek philosophers brought into the Church (see Chapter 9).

The answer to our question about Christ's delay to earth is found in Scripture. Christ is certainly coming back to establish a kingdom on the earth according to the Bible, but this concept goes against Greek myths that came into Christian culture. However, we find answers within the context of the Old Testament (O.T.) bringing the same terms into the N.T.

When we see phrases like "no more delay" or "I am coming soon" in the N.T., we need to consider the full meaning as drawn from the O.T. The answers are found after we follow the breadcrumbs.

### Isaiah 46:8-13

*"Remember this and stand firm,*
*recall it to mind, you transgressors,*
*remember the former things of old;*
*for I am God, and there is no other;*

*I am God, and there is none like me,*
*declaring the end from the beginning and*
*from ancient times things not yet done, saying,*
*'My counsel shall stand,*
*and I will accomplish all my purpose,'*
*... I have spoken, and I will bring it to pass;*
*I have purposed, and I will do it.*
*Listen to me, you stubborn of heart,*
*you who are far from righteousness:*

*I bring near my righteousness; it is not far off,*
*and **my salvation will not delay**;*
*I will put salvation in Zion, for Israel my glory."*

> Isaiah 10:20-23 *"In that day the remnant of Israel and the survivors of the house of Jacob will no more lean on him who struck them, but will lean on the LORD, the Holy One of Israel, in truth. A remnant will return, the remnant of Jacob, to the mighty God. For though your people Israel be as the sand of the sea, only a remnant of them will return. Destruction is decreed, overflowing with righteousness. For the Lord GOD of hosts will make a full end, as decreed, in the midst of all the earth."*

Paul stated in Romans 9 that the timing mentioned by Isaiah is yet future. We also see his reference to the prophetic "non-delayed" theme about the second advent.

> Romans 9:27-28 *"And Isaiah cries out concerning Israel: 'Though the number of the sons of Israel be as the sand of the sea, only a remnant of them will be saved, for the Lord will carry out his sentence upon the earth fully and **without delay**.'"*

In Hebrews 10 we notice a reference to Habakkuk 2:3. First, the Savior comes, then He will act quickly when He comes.

> Hebrews 10:36-37 *"For you have need of endurance, so that when you have done the will of God you may receive what is promised. For, 'Yet a little while, and the coming one will come and **will not delay**;'"*

> Revelation 10:5-7 *"And the angel whom I saw standing on the sea and on the land raised his right hand to heaven and swore by him who lives forever and ever, who created heaven and what is in it, the earth and what is in it, and the sea and what is in it, that there would be **no more delay**, but that in the days of the trumpet call to be sounded by the seventh angel, **the mystery of God would be fulfilled**, just as he announced to his servants the prophets."*

No more delay? There has been a huge delay from our perspective, but God's timing is not our timing. The ancient language seems to have been misunderstood by our modern terms. He knows exactly when all things will come to pass. What does He want us to learn about this? We will later examine how God's timing is tied to hope. There is a sense that these prophecies give us what we need to live today, while knowing what the future holds.

Ezekiel 12 states a correlation of the term "delay" to occur in far-off days, yet that these days are "near" (not in terms of time). People usually think of things happening in the near future to be in a matter of

> Ezekiel 12:23-28 *And the word of the LORD came to me: "Son of man, what is this proverb that you have about the land of Israel, saying, 'The days grow long, and every vision comes to nothing'? Tell them therefore, 'Thus says the Lord GOD: I will put an end to this proverb, and they shall no more use it as a proverb in Israel.' But say to them,* **The days are near***, and the fulfillment of every vision. For there shall be no more any false vision or flattering divination within the house of Israel. For I am the LORD; I will speak the word that I will speak, and it will be performed.* **It will no longer be delayed***, but in your days, O rebellious house, I will speak the word and perform it, declares the Lord GOD."*
>
> *And the word of the LORD came to me: "Son of man, behold, they of the house of Israel say, 'The vision that he sees is for many days from now, and he prophesies of times far off.' Therefore say to them, Thus says the Lord GOD: None of my words will be delayed any longer,* **but the word that I speak will be performed***, declares the Lord GOD."*

days. Our commons conceptions of time within the scope of our lives are woefully insufficient to easily grasp the prophetic meaning of time that these statements refer to. Put your goggles and scuba flippers on. Let's dive into the language of time as it appears in the Bible.

Notice that our modern meaning and the context meaning of "delay" are not the same. The biblical meaning of delay in these prophetic passages is that God will certainly carry out His will where it is not far off or something to be forgotten. He decided to act, so all prophecies will be fulfilled. Even though it may be thousands of years in advance, it will not "come to nothing."

We can be assured by God's word, even when spoken thousands of years ago. It is not far removed from us because time is not the same in eternity (2 Peter 3:8). When God speaks, it is if the event He planned already occurred. Also, when prophesied events finally occur, they will happen quickly. "Delay" is not a simple term with a short answer.

The naysayers of Ezekiel's time thought the timing of God's prophecies and promises were "growing long" or stretching out farther. God replied they were incorrect. His prophecies were nearer or closer than they thought. He already established timing of fulfillment. They thought He kept pushing back the countdown to postpone His promises.

Habakkuk 2:2-3

*And the LORD answered me:*

15

*"Write the vision; make it plain on tablets,*
*so he may run who reads it.*
*For still the vision awaits its appointed time;*
*it hastens to the end—it will not lie.*
*If it seems slow, wait for it;*
*it will surely come; **it will not delay.**"*

Both Habakkuk and Ezekiel stated that God's promises will surely happen. This is the main point of these passages relating to the "delay" term. They were not meant to occur immediate to the time of the prophecy.

Now that we have some background from the O.T., we notice similar timing terms carry over into the N.T.

> Luke 18:6-8 *And the Lord said, "Hear what the unrighteous judge says. And will not God give justice to his elect, who cry to him day and night? Will he delay long over them? I tell you, **he will give justice to them speedily.** Nevertheless, when the Son of Man comes, will he find faith on earth?"*

2 Peter 3:1-7 *"This is now the second letter that I am writing to you, beloved. In both of them I am stirring up your sincere mind by way of reminder, that you should remember the predictions of the holy prophets and the commandment of the Lord and Savior through your apostles, knowing this first of all, that scoffers will come in the last days with scoffing, following their own sinful desires. They will say, 'Where is the promise of his coming? For ever since the fathers fell asleep, all things are continuing as they were from the beginning of creation.' For they deliberately overlook this fact, that the heavens existed long ago, and the earth was formed out of water and through water by the word of God, and that by means of these the world that then existed was deluged with water and perished. But by the same word the heavens and earth that now exist are stored up for fire, being kept until the day of judgment and destruction of the ungodly."*

Scoffers will not know when the end will come. It is because of sin that they will not know. There is a definite correlation of knowledge of God's certain word of prophecy only being revealed to the righteous (wise, just). Simply reading Bible prophecies or even understanding the original language is not enough according to the Bible itself. Good works follow understanding the Bible through the reception of His word by His Spirit. God grants true knowledge of His future revelations to those who are righteous.

Prophecies about Christ coming soon stem from the original prophecies that Moses wrote. There are early prophecies about Christ as the expected Savior mentioned in Genesis 3:15 and Genesis 22:17-18. However, within the Song of Moses we receive the first glimpse about the means of the Lord's coming.

> Deuteronomy 32:35 *Vengeance is mine, and recompense, for the time when their foot shall slip; for the day of their calamity is at hand, and their doom comes* ***swiftly***.

It should be noted that all passages we reviewed about timing stem from the Song of Moses. This hope of justice upon the evil of the earth was ingrained into God's people and repeated by several prophets and apostles.

Terms like recompense and swiftness appear again and again, misleadingly giving the impression of something that is bound to happen imminently. Later prophets built upon previous terms so that the hearer or reader can trace the contextual meaning, simply creating a sequence of events rather than codifying their proximity to one another. They followed the Song of Moses as a basis but did not repeat the entire prophecy. They often added new information to the base prophecy.

The book of Revelation serves as a greatest-hits record, playing mostly repeats of previous prophecies. We will not understand the final book of the Bible if we don't understand the origins of these threads, such as the Song of Moses to Isaiah to Christ to John. Perhaps unsurprisingly, God wants us to read and understand all of Scripture, not just parts. Surprisingly, there are not many new concepts found in the prophecies mentioned in Revelation when we apply this threaded breadcrumb approach.

The concept of the Song of Moses prophecy is repeated by Isaiah in several passages, including Isaiah 35:4 and Isaiah 62:11 stated here –

> *Behold, the LORD has proclaimed*
> *to the end of the earth:*
> *Say to the daughter of Zion,*
> *Behold, your salvation comes;*
> *behold, his reward is with him,*
> *and his recompense before him.*

When we go back to examine Revelation 22, we have a better understanding that "coming soon" is tied to recompense and swift judgment. This is based upon this Song of Moses and related prophesies in Isaiah. "Coming soon" means quick in relation to judgment upon the earth.

Revelation 22:12 *"Behold, I am coming soon, bringing my recompense with me, to repay each one for what he has done."*

The message of the prophetic gospel is clear, as we will examine through this book. The Church, Christians, and blood descendants of Israel will be on earth during tribulation and the Great Tribulation Period. There is no avoiding this with a secret or public rapture prior to this coming period. However, the righteous are not destined for God's wrath. Wrath and tribulation are different terms. We need to understand that believers will enter tribulation but not wrath.

1 Thessalonians 5:2-4 *"For you yourselves are fully aware that the day of the Lord will come like a thief in the night. While people are saying, 'There is peace and security,' then sudden destruction will come upon them as labor pains come upon a pregnant woman, and they will not escape. But you are not in darkness, brothers, for that day to surprise you like a thief. For you are all children of light, children of the day. We are not of the night or of the darkness."*

## Key Takeaways from 1 Thessalonians 5

**Wise** = righteous = God's word believed = in the light = spared from wrath

**Unwise** = unrighteous = reject God's word = in darkness = destined to wrath

1 Thessalonians 5 makes it clear for us. We need to be prepared for the coming great judgment upon the earth. There will be no surprise for believers, only unbelievers will be surprised how quickly events will occur.

All types of people will be on earth during dark times, but hope is offered to all who believe in God's final message to us. We are given this hope a little later in 1 Thessalonians 5:9. Not to worry, everything that we need to know was written for us in advance as He "declared the end from the beginning."

# Chapter 18

## *When Do the Events of Revelation Occur?*

Another modern display of confusion is the coming end of the world that is not really the end of the world. This eye-opening realization instead signals the end of the age in which we live. The earth will be cleansed at that time, washed clean of evil, false prophets, and those who turned away from God. After cleansing, there will be an eternal age on earth ("Heaven" will be revealed on earth). The unseen spiritual subtext of our lives will become realized in our physical space at the merger of Heaven and earth (Ephesians 1:10).

To understand Revelation, we need to have a starting point as a marker to guide us through all the events. The main marker is a grouping of the Big 3 events. They are closely associated with timing to the end of our age (just prior to the next age).

The Big 3 events listed below should be considered first as guideposts to understand sequencing of events in Revelation. Clear passages must dictate the unclear. Big 3 passages with two or three events mentioned in one passage show groupings of associated events at the same timing. See Chapter 6 for detailed information.

Christ comes again to earth, then the resurrection of the dead and judgment of individuals occur on earth. Other events before and after the second coming are more complex. However, if we start with the Big 3 cluster, we can place other events more easily in terms of details, location, and timing.

Philippians 3:20-21 *"But our citizenship is in Heaven, and from it* **we await** *a Savior, the Lord Jesus* **Christ, who will transform our lowly body to be like his glorious body,** *by the power that enables him even to subject all things to himself."* This passage correlates to Luke 20:35-36.

The resurrection includes transformation of the saints at the second advent. All spirits of the saints kept with Christ (now at rest) and all alive saints on earth receive new bodies at this one event. The resting saints are raised first, then saints on earth are transformed, so all believers from all time are in one place.

One of the first questions to ask is – why would Christ bring spirits of the saints with Him here to earth? Why not just meet them in Heaven? The reason is that all saints are going to live with immortal bodies on earth. See Chapter 7 and other chapters in this book showing that "Heaven" will be merged with the newly restored earth.

## Common Themes During the Second Advent

1 Thessalonians 4 depicts an archangel, a trumpet, a voice, and clouds at the second coming and resurrection events. These events are prior to judgment and correlate to Matthew 24:30-31. Similar passages contain identical elements – Daniel 7:13; Matthew 13:24-43, 16:27; Mark 8:38; Luke 21:27; John 5:28; 1 Corinthians 15:52; Philippians 3:14; 2 Thessalonians 1:7; Jude 1:14-15; Revelation 1:7, 14:14, 19:11-14.

There is only one second coming – rapture event. More information can be found in our "Post-tribulation Rapture" article on Academia.edu and in chapters 23 and 24 of this book.

This meeting of all believers spares the living saints on earth from God's final wrath being poured out at the end of this age. Christ will cleanse and harvest the earth when He comes as we see in Joel 3:12-16, Luke 17:26-37, Matthew 13:24-30, 36-43, 2 Peter 3:7-14 and as described in two chapters of Revelation retelling the same events in Revelation 14:14-20 and Revelation 19:11-21 (these two sections of Revelation are parallel in timing that are described differently, but are not different events).

The Great Tribulation period and other events in Revelation are complex. We can simplify time sequences with correlations such as Christ destroying the final beast of the antichrist at His return. See Revelation 19:19-20 compared to Daniel 7:11-26 and 2 Thessalonians 2:1-9 that depicts destruction timing at the second coming. These correlations depend on a literal interpretation (i.e., a real man, not a spiritual antichrist).

## Passages Describing Antichrist's Destruction

Daniel 7:11, 22, 26 = 2 Thessalonians 2:8 = Revelation 14:14-20, 17:14, 19:19-20

Before the return of Christ, we see another association to the Book of Revelation where the final antichrist is speaking great abominations. He exalts himself as god and sets up the final, false worship system.

## Passages About the Abomination of Desolation

Daniel 7:8, 11, 25 = Matthew 24:15 = 2 Thessalonians 2:3-4 = Revelation 13:5-6

There are many other correlations such as when the antichrist is granted authority by God and is allowed to conquer the saints for a short time during the tribulation period. This occurs at the same time that the devil is cast to earth as his beast system rises (Revelation 13:1).

## The Devil Makes War Through the Antichrist

Daniel 7:21-22 = Revelation 12:17 = Revelation 13:7

Assistance to understand Revelation's sequencing of events comes from ample support in other passages and concepts throughout the Bible. Sometimes, to get the most out of a recent cover song, we need to go back to the original artist so we learn the progression. These progressing passages show their timing connections to Revelation.

A key end-time chapter is 1 Corinthians 15. This chapter provides details of the relationships between the second advent and bodily resurrection timing to coincide with the reign period of Revelation 20 that we need to learn more about.

## 1 Corinthians 15 Timing Correlations

1 Corinthians 15:23 = Daniel 7:22 = Matthew 24:30 = Revelation1:7, 14:1, 19:11 (second advent)

1 Corinthians 15:24 = Revelation 11:15-18 (Christ begins His reign on earth at the 7th trumpet)

1 Corinthians 15:25 = Revelation 20:4-7 (Christ reigns on earth before death is destroyed)

1 Corinthians 15:26 = Revelation 20:14 (death is defeated).

1 Corinthians 15:23-26 lays out the order of events. Christ comes as stated in 15:23; He completes His reign in 15:24-25; then death is destroyed in 15:26 after the reign when He hands over the kingdom. This outline can be used to understand chapters 19 & 20 of Revelation that describe these same events.

To understand end times and Revelation, we need to realize that everything revolves around the second coming of Christ (a single event, not multiple appearances of a rapture and a separate, final coming).

Acts 1:11 is very clear. Christ is coming back again (literally / physically). All end-time events hinge upon the second advent.

> Acts 1:11b *This Jesus, who was taken up from you into heaven, will come in the same way as you saw him go into heaven.*

Acts 1:11 = 1 Corinthians 15:23 and all related verses of a single, second advent. There are no secret raptures or other future appearances of Christ in the Bible. Only one return is referenced, with signs correlated that we will explore in Chapter 24.

It may look like Christ comes back multiple times in Revelation, but it is one event. Revelation 14:1 = 19:11. Revelation is non-linear in timing and circular in that it often repeats previous events.

We will see how to easily identify "out of sequence" passages so we can correlate and place them into a linear timeline. This important concept can be understood by using the Big 3 events as our end the age marker, while adding details from the 7 seals of Revelation compared to Matthew 24.

# Chapter 19

*What Are the 7 Seals of Revelation?*

## Matthew 24 Explains the 7 Seals

One of the foremost symbols we'll be analyzing, the 7 seals of Revelation chapters 6 and 8 provide a wide-view lens of the end of this age. They go hand in hand with our understanding of the Bible's prophetic timeline, guiding us with an overall perspective to track a course through the complex chapters of the book.

Revelation is not chronological, but the 7 seals are consecutive with their timing. They are an exact parallel to Christ's famous age-ending prophecies found in Matthew 24.

Please see <u>Appendix 3</u> for a side-by-side comparison of Revelation chapters 6 and 8 as they correlate to passages in Matthew 24. This overview helps us understand the beginning of end-time trials, through the Great Tribulation Period, which Christ states in Matthew 24 <u>verse 21</u> as the worst era of earth's history.

The first seal is opened by Christ to allow a rider, depicted on a white horse, to conquer the earth. This parallels Matthew 24 verse 5 regarding false messiahs. Messiahs can be religious or political saviors, but these end-time false messiahs depict a complete world system as they set out to conquer both domains. This is the preparation phase, the beginning of the end. There is no turning back the clock once the white horse is released.

The second seal begins end-time wars with reports, then escalation. It follows along with Matthew 24 verses 6 and 7. This is not Armageddon, since there will be a lot more events yet to come. These wars will create a sense of global distress.

The third seal is about famines coinciding with Matthew 24 verse 7. We can certainly imagine what the earth with be like when food is scarce. There will be more fighting and distress. What will Christians be doing during this time? Hopefully, we will help our neighbor.

The fourth seal results in deaths from the wars and famines mentioned in Matthew 24:7-8. By the time the fourth seal is completed, it will look like the end of the world. The world will be ready for its savior, not Christ.

The Abomination of Desolation occurs at the time of the fifth seal, as inferred by following the parallel text in Matthew 24:15-27. This is the mid-point of Daniel's 70th week, when the devil claims to be the true god through the person of the antichrist. If we think the first four seals are going to be bad, we are going to have a rude awakening about what comes next.

## The 5th Seal Depicts Martyrs

The fifth seal begins the Great Tribulation Period. The Church will go through this awful time. The details and results are stated in Mathew 24:9, Revelation 13:10 and Revelation 20:4-6. Martyrdom, and believers entering captivity, are results of the antichrist's war with the saints mentioned in Daniel 7:21-26 and Revelation 13:5-10. Not all of God's chosen people will be persecuted; some will be divinely protected by being sealed (Revelation 7:3-4) or they will be carried on eagle's wings (Revelation 12:14).

The sixth seal begins the Day of the Lord after the antichrist exalts himself above all gods and proclaims to be God (2 Thessalonians 2:3-4). There are many references to the Day of the Lord, such as Matthew 24:29-30 and Revelation 6:12-17 that parallel Joel 3:9-16, Isaiah 2:12-22 and Isaiah 34:4 with the same Day of the Lord signs.

The seventh seal closes out the age we live in with Christ emerging from the veil of the heavenly realm to begin His physical reign on earth.

Matthew 24:30-31 occurs at the timing of the seventh seal when there is silence in Heaven (Revelation 8:1). All prayers are answered (Revelation 8:3-5) at the climax of the Day of the Lord. This occurs at the end of time, just before the merger of Heaven and earth. Christ comes to earth!

The seventh seal begins the process of the second coming and the rapture. This is the resurrection of the dead and the beginning of the next age (1 Corinthians 15:22-26). It is the start of the invisible realm being revealed on the newly restored earth where Christ will dwell after He cleanses it (2 Peter 3:12-13).

# Chapter 20

## Will Christians Go Through the Great Tribulation Period?

The Church (Messianic Jews and Gentiles) will go through the greatest tribulation ever known, as will blood-Israel descendants. Without true believers facing the adversity of this cataclysmic event, there would be no need for warnings to the 7 Churches (including us today) not to take the Mark of the Beast, or that we may die by the sword, or go into captivity. Revelation 13:9-10 is clear that this is written for the saints. The context depicts saints on earth during the Great Tribulation Period.

The Book of Revelation was not written for people who will not understand it, yet alone read it. There is no scenario hinted in the Bible that the Church will be raptured and leave a bunch of Bibles behind for unbelievers to read during the worst period of earth's history. The warnings of Revelation are made directly to people who will head them (us). The other group mentioned will not repent during this time (Revelation 9:20-21).

End-time events prior to Christ's return to earth revolve around a critical and often-referenced 3.5 year period that we'll dig through in close detail. Despite what others have suggested, this is not likely to be an extended period over the entire Church age. Even though we have been in the latter days of the age since apostolic times (Hebrews 1:1-2), the past 2,000 years have not been the end times.

Revelation 3:10 speaks to a short period on the earth. Satan will only be given a moment by God, granting him authority to wreak havoc upon the earth. Satan will then grant all his authority to his final beast system that the antichrist comes out of. We will study this authority in future chapters.

Revelation 12:12 depicts the short time satan will have after Michael's war in verse 7 (which is within the same timing of Michael mentioned in Daniel 12:1). This is also the same period as removal of the restrainer that Paul mentions in 2 Thessalonians 2:1-12, although he does not mention Michael by name. The time periods Paul speaks of, and key points about the antichrist, match with Daniel, so we can confidently assume that Paul was speaking of Michael as the restrainer. Paul obviously knew the book of Daniel very well, as Paul's key concepts are derived from Daniel and Christ. Paul was not given any new prophecy in this chapter since there was no new information provided.

We should realize these events occur over a modest period of time. They are not constrained to one day, but they do not happen over thousands of years either.

## Michael as the Restrainer

Michael defeats satan in Heaven so that satan's spirit is loose on the earth and allowed a short time of authority over the earth.

This equals satan's release from restrainment timing, where Michael is a key figure that helps to launch the Great Tribulation Period while protecting God's chosen people through these events.

Why does Michael let the devil loose? This would probably prevent the Great Tribulation Period from happening. The answer is revealed in God's plan for the end of this age.

The War in Heaven results in the creation of conflict here on earth, after God allows satan authority to spread evil.

Daniel 12:1 shows that Michael "stands up" or "arises." This sounds like he is fighting for Israel at first, yet there is the greatest trouble for the saints ever known mentioned after he stands up. He "stands aside" for a short time to let the devil loose since he is no longer the restrainer. However, Michael stands for Israel to protect them.

*Daniel 12:1 At that time shall arise Michael, the great prince who has charge of your people. And there shall be a time of trouble, such as never has been since there was a nation till that time. But at that time your people shall be delivered, everyone whose name shall be found written in the book.*

Daniel 12:1 delivers the knockout blow when it comes to comprehending the significance of this 3.5 year period when the devil is kicked out of Heaven and allowed to wreak havoc during the Great Tribulation. At present, he is allowed access to Heaven and on earth but is restrained from total access. There will be more to come about satan's location and authority at each location he is known to be in.

Daniel 12:2 locates the timing of Revelation chapters 19-20 within the circumstances of the resurrection occurring at Christ's coming. This Daniel 12:1-2 scenario shows the Great Tribulation after Michael stands up (kicks satan out of Heaven, then stands aside to let satan roam the earth freely via his spiritual kingdom of the beast and antichrist). Afterward, Christ comes to save his people via the resurrection of the dead and transformation of those living on earth, harkening in the time of His kingdom of Heaven. Daniel 12:1-2 can be considered as an approximately 3.5 year period, a length of time that appears again and again throughout Daniel and Revelation.

Christ referenced the prophecies of Daniel in Matthew 24, starting in verse 15. This entire section is summarized in verse 21 –

*For then there will be great tribulation, such as has not been from the beginning of the world until now, no, and never will be.*

Christ said that if the Great Tribulation Period is not shortened, nobody will be saved. This is the transition from this awful time created by the beast and his followers to the Day of the Lord, which we will examine later in relation to God's wrath upon the earth.

Matthew 24:22 *And if those days had not been cut short, no human being would be saved. But for the sake of the elect those days will be cut short.*

You can imagine that with Satan's spirit loose on the earth that "all hell will break out." If Christ does not come back to defeat this beast, God's people would perish without the restrainer watching over. God allows tribulation, but He always has a greater salvation plan. We do not need to worry since 1 Thessalonians 5:9 states that we are not destined for God's wrath.

While their meanings in lay terms might carry plenty of overlap, tribulation and wrath are different terms that carry widely disparate significances and uses. His wrath is directed at the unrighteous, but He allows saints to go through tribulations.

Why would God allow subject his most faithful followers to a period of hardship and suffering? He does this to show His great mercy so that grace may abound. Is this too simple of an answer? See <u>Romans 9:14-24</u> and <u>Romans 11:25-33</u>. The apostle Paul thinks that God's will yields the greatest display of His mercy. God's will is at the heart of it all, even the greatest adversity any of us will ever experience.

> <u>Proverbs 16:4</u> *The LORD has made everything for its purpose, even the wicked for the day of trouble.*

Regardless of how we may feel about the struggles of our time, the greatest trials lie in wait for us in the future, but we can take profound comfort that the greatest outpouring of grace will be realized for all Israel (blood descendants of Abraham and the Gentiles to form the entire Church) at the end of the age. Nothing short of eternal life and complete salvation hang in the balance.

*1 Thessalonians 2:4 but just as we have been approved by God to be entrusted with the gospel, so we speak, not to please man, but to please God who tests our hearts.*

*James 1:12 Blessed is the man who remains steadfast under trial, for when he has stood the test he will receive the crown of life, which God has promised to those who love him.*

*2 Peter 2:9 then the Lord knows how to rescue the godly from trials, and to keep the unrighteous under punishment until the day of judgment,*

*Revelation 3:10 Because you have kept my word about patient endurance, I will keep you from the hour of trial that is coming on the whole world, to try those who dwell on the earth.*

We will be spared from the greatest trial like Israel was spared the plagues in Egypt.

*Romans 5:9 Since, therefore, we have now been justified by his blood, much more shall we be saved by him from the wrath of God.*

Revelation 7:3 *"saying, 'Do not harm the earth or the sea or the trees, until we have sealed the servants of our God on their foreheads.'"*

Revelation 15:1 *Then I saw another sign in heaven, great and amazing, seven angels with seven plagues, which are the last, for with them the wrath of God is finished.*

Believers escape God's wrath. The Day of the Lord is focused upon unbelievers – Revelation 14:9-10, Revelation 16:1-2. However, there is Divine protection for the saints.

Revelation 9:4 *They were told not to harm the grass of the earth or any green plant or any tree, but only those people who do not have the seal of God on their foreheads.*

Paul provides meaning about the Day of the Lord in 1 Thessalonians 5:1-10 that we need to consider. The children of light are to be prepared for this day, but the children of darkness will be surprised. This passage parallels Peter's passage about the coming Day of the Lord and those who are not expecting it (2 Peter 3:3-4).

These passages convey the difference between believers (those who are wise) compared to unbelievers (the unwise). This is like Daniel 12:8-10 and 2 Thessalonians 2:10-12 stating the same concepts as Peter about people living in the last days. Peter and Paul derived their learning from Daniel and Christ.

## Is There an Imminent Pre-Trib Rapture?

This brings up the concept of a surprise coming of Christ. Imminence of Christ's return is not mentioned in scripture. There is not a single verse of Christ coming at any moment as a surprise to believers. Where is the supporting passage? Instead, passages speak of being prepared and to look for the signs.

The human concept of surprise is when someone turns on the lights and people jump out from hiding places then yell, "happy birthday!" A surprise happens in an instant. It is not a long, drawn-out event. Only unbelievers and the unrepentant would be surprised, as in Revelation 1:7.

The onset of a 3.5 year tribulation period will not be a surprise for believers, because there will be false signs and wonders during this period as time stamps. Unbelievers will seek a false god to save them during these false events. This is another recognizable sign of the coming antichrist for those who keep faith and refuse to be led astray. God will allow all groups to be subject to the ultimate test of human history, since everyone will see the same signs. Only the wise and righteous will understand that the events will be more than just a societal tumult.

Judgement will be swift and without delay, as mentioned in Isaiah 46:13, Hebrews 10:37 and Romans 9:27-28. The unwise will be shocked when they see Christ, since they will have rejected Him, scoffed at Him, etc. The wise will look at scripture and the signs, so they will not be surprised at all. We will be given hope to make it through great tribulations while in captivity, or we will be given hope in martyrdom.

Matthew 24:15, 24:33, Luke 21:31, and Mark 13:29 repeat the same message to look with eyes to see these events. We know these passages are speaking of physical eyes, since the same root words are used for Christ's first advent. There is no hint of using metaphors about spiritual eyesight. John has a beautiful summary about this in terms of future timing and literal eyesight.

> 1 John 3:2 *Beloved, we are God's children now, and what we will be has not yet appeared; but we know that **when he appears** we shall be like him, because **we shall see him as he is**.*

43

Those who are easily manipulated and love sin will fall for these false signs and wonders, some having never encountered the biblical prophecies telling them about these events in advance. Everything relating to the true signs written thousands of years ago will not matter even for those unbelievers who cannot see them. Between turning away from the word of God and the open acceptance of sin, a large percentage of the people who occupy society with us will follow false signs before the final signs of the Day of the Lord come. They will believe lies they want to hear, even when the truth is staring them in the face.

The bottom line is that God will allow people to worship a final false god, just as He has allowed the freedom to reject Him and follow false gods in the past, except it will be on the grandest scale in the future. We dislike thinking about God granting authority to satan or letting angels harm people or the earth but He has done it, does it, and will do it again to show His wisdom even if we do not fully understand His reasoning yet. It is about the greatest test ever to complete this age, to prove His grace, and to save as many as possible.

> <u>James 1:2-3</u> *Count it all joy, my brothers, when you meet trials of various kinds, for you know that the testing of your faith produces steadfastness.*

44

1 Peter 1:6-7 *In this you rejoice, though now for a little while, if necessary, you have been grieved by various trials, so that the tested genuineness of your faith—more precious than gold that perishes though it is tested by fire—may be found to result in praise and glory and honor at the revelation of Jesus Christ.*

Revelation 2:10 *Do not fear what you are about to suffer. Behold, the devil is about to throw some of you into prison, that you may be tested, and for ten days you will have tribulation. Be faithful unto death, and I will give you the crown of life.*

# Chapter 21

## *What Is the Abomination of Desolation?*

The great harbinger prior to the Great Tribulation Period is the antichrist rising up to espouse great abominations, the most heinous of which being that he will exalt himself as god to begin the greatest false worship system ever known.

### Passages About the Abomination of Desolation

Daniel 7:8, 11, 25 = Matthew 24:15 = 2 Thessalonians 2:3-4 = Revelation 13:5-6

He speaks, acts out, and commits great atrocities on behalf of the final beast of the end-times (we will explore the details of this beast in Chapter 28). Being empowered by the devil's spirit of this beast, we see God grant permission to allow the unholy trinity to conquer the saints (Daniel 7:21 = Revelation 13:7).

In 2 Thessalonians 2:3-4 we see the antichrist taking away all other forms of worship and replacing all other religions. He makes the greatest statement that he is god. This will be the time where he cuts off worship at the temple (or tabernacle) in Jerusalem, the famous mid-point of Daniel's 70th week. It is the period that other false religions are also cut off (Revelation 17:16), so it is not only sacrifices of the Jews that are suspended.

Daniel chapters 2, 7 and 12 are easier to understand so we can establish a background about the abomination. Let's skip ahead to chapter 12 of Daniel to see the ending summary that the angel gave to Daniel before we return to the difficult section about the 70 weeks prophecy.

> Daniel 12:11-12 *"And from the time that the regular burnt offering is taken away and the abomination that makes desolate is set up, there shall be 1,290 days. Blessed is he who waits and arrives at the 1,335 days."*

Much comfort can be taken from this heartening summary at the end of Daniel about the beginning and ending of the Great Tribulation Period, but it doesn't help put all the pieces together by itself. There are still unresolved questions and the fate of many hanging in the balance.

Christ also mentioned this abomination, so let's see what He had to say in the Olivet Discourse. Matthew 24:14-29 is placed in this crucial timing area.

Verse 14 describes what happens prior to the abomination. This is the age in which we now live (the time of the Gentiles). The gospel message of the kingdom age established on earth needs to be preached to the entire world before the end will come.

> Matthew 24:14 *"And **this gospel of the kingdom** will be proclaimed throughout the whole world as a testimony to all nations, and then the end will come."*

Verse 15 references Daniel's prophecy as our starting point of the Great Tribulation Period kicked off by the Abomination of Desolation.

> Matthew 24:15 *"So when **you** see the abomination of desolation spoken of by the prophet Daniel, standing in the holy place..."*

Who is "you"? This is who Christ called the "generation" mentioned in Matthew 24:34 (similar to Luke 21:32). The generation of people means Israel at any point in time, as referenced in Matthew 23 (see Chapter 1 for more information, but it is clear Christ was not talking about his disciples seeing the abomination event in 70 AD.) Matthew 23 provides clear meaning of the same root-term "generation" context of Matthew 24 so the disciples know that the people of Israel will exist to see the last days.

Verse 15 calls out to us loud and clear in terms of our role to recognize that Scripture is the vehicle delivering a message directly to us thousands of years later. *"Let the reader understand."* This means the intent is for the reader, not the apostle who wrote it down or an early audience since they would not be alive during the greatest tribulation. This statement ties into wisdom mentioned in Daniel 12:8-10, 2 Thessalonians 2:10-12, Revelation 13:18, and 17:9-10.

Verses 16 through 20 of Matthew 24 get into the details – *"then let those who are in Judea flee to the mountains…"* First, the generation of "Israel" living in the end times needs to see the abomination. Then they are to flee, as wrath is about to be poured out onto the earth. This passage is very similar to Luke 21 of His Temple Mount message where Christ spoke of destruction of the second temple in 70 AD. The Temple Mount message was not the Olivet Discourse in Matthew 24 and Mark 13. Luke 21 was a different message given at a different time and location (on the Temple Mount, not the Mount of Olives as was stated in Matthew 24 and Mark 13).

Luke 21:24 mentions destruction of the second temple in relation to the times of the Gentiles beginning. Matthew 24:14 speaks to the time of spreading the gospel throughout the earth before the final abomination occurs. Matthew reported that the abomination will not occur until after the gospel is spread, so there is an association of the times of the Gentiles to the spread of the yet-to-come kingdom gospel.

There have been abominations in the past but there is only one final, great abomination, which is a focal point of the seventy weeks prophecy of Daniel 9 and related passages speaking of the same event – Daniel 7:8, 11, 25 = Daniel 12:11-12 = Matthew 24:15 = 2 Thessalonians 2:3-4 = Revelation 13:5-6

Verse 21 of Matthew 24 states, *"For then there will be great tribulation, such as has not been from the beginning of the world until now, no, and never will be."*

Therefore, people will need to leave Judea (like the warning prior to the AD 70 event that was described in Luke 21). There are similar statements to Matthew 24:21 in Jeremiah 30:7, Daniel 12:1 and Joel 2:2. It is the greatest tribulation in human history. The holocaust or destruction of the second temple by the Romans do not match the events described in the prophecies at the end of this age.

The key timing association is verse 15 of Matthew 24 stating "when" with association to verse 21 stating "then." "When" the abomination is seen "then" there will be great tribulation. This leads into verse 22 with "those days" (meaning a shortened Great Tribulation Period).

Verse 22 states, *"And if those days had not been cut short, no human being would be saved. But for the sake of the elect those days will be cut short."*

It is most unlikely that this statement refers to the 70 AD destruction of the second temple by the Romans, since those people mentioned in Luke 21 were simply warned to flee Judea before that time. There would have been no need for cutting days short, since these people of the Luke 21:21-22 reference simply migrated away to other countries, as shown throughout history by the Church spreading out (away from Jerusalem). However, great tribulation days will be cut short in the future.

Verses 23-26 of Matthew 24 provide the same warnings of false signs and wonders as in 2 Thessalonians 2:9 and Revelation 13:13. The beast, its image, and the false prophet are connected to the authority of Satan. *"Then if anyone says to you, 'Look, here is the Christ!' or 'There he is!' do not believe it. For false Christs and false prophets will arise and perform great signs and wonders, so as to lead astray, if possible, even the elect..."*

The progressing of events is unmistakable, beginning with the coming of the abomination, the rise of this false religious system and false god, and then leading to its acceptance by masses of unbelievers. These followers will be part of demonic activity and will perform false signs. Authority is granted from God > satan > beast > antichrist and many who will worship satan will be granted authority to perform false wonders. Revelation 16:13-14 shows where the ability to do signs comes from. It is by demonic activity like this example to sway the kings of the earth to fight against God during the 6th bowl judgment period that we will discuss more about later.

In Matthew 24:24, we can see the elect is still on earth (otherwise, they could not be deceived). This is another reason that there is no pre-trib rapture, as the Church is always mentioned as being on earth in the Olivet Discourse, Thessalonians, and the book of Revelation. The elect are not gathered until Matthew 24:31 at the second advent.

We see in verse 27 of Matthew 24 that *"For as the lightning comes from the east and shines as far as the west, so will be the coming of the Son of Man."* It will be visible for all to see when the real second coming occurs, like in Isaiah 40:5, Revelation 1:7 and related second advent appearance passages. Before that great event will be a counterfeit messiah and counterfeit signs presented. We are to be wise so we do not fall into satan's traps, as mentioned in Matthew 24:24.

Verse 29 transitions this important passage into the actual second coming itself. *"**Immediately** after the tribulation of those days..."* Christ comes right after the Great Tribulation period. There is never any verse that states Christ comes before tribulation to save the elect. Instead, we are told we need to have patience, even if it means death or captivity. Also, see <u>Revelation 13:9-10</u>. Perhaps now, considering these dire warnings and catastrophic threats, we can better understand Daniel's prophecy in <u>12:12</u> about being blessed for waiting until the 1335th day.

We are now ready to learn about detailed time sequences since we have a general understanding about the Abomination of Desolation that begins the Great Tribulation Period and the following events. We will plunge into Daniel chapters 2, 7, 9 and 12, along with their associations to the beast and antichrist, in the coming chapters.

# Chapter 22

## What Is the Sequence of Events in Revelation?

### Birth Pains Describe the End-times

The Bible presages the coming of end times with an unusually visceral phrase, referring to the onset of this period as "birth pangs." There is a clear association of signs leading up to the second advent that intensify until their inevitable culmination. This intensification conveys an increase from initial signs that result in "mild" tribulation, to the final outpouring of God's wrath with the most terrifying depictions.

> Matthew 24:8 *All these are but the beginning of the birth pains.*

These birth pangs are shown from seals to trumpets to bowl judgments in Revelation, and their magnitude becomes apparent when we examine one term like "earthquake."

## Correlations of the 7th Seal, Trumpet and Bowl

**7th Seal** – describes *"an earthquake"*

**7th Trumpet** – describes *"an earthquake and heavy hail"*

**7th Bowl** – describes *"a great earthquake such as there had never been since man was on the earth, so great was that earthquake... And great hailstones, about one hundred pounds each, fell from heaven on people; and they cursed God for the plague of the hail, because the plague was so severe."*

Seals are opened by Christ to begin the end of the age. Trumpets announce the wrath of God coming from Heaven to earth. Bowls complete God's judgment upon the earth during the Day of the Lord period.

Let's examine the language from the 7th seal being opened to the 7th bowl being poured out.

*Revelation 8:1 When the Lamb opened the seventh seal, there was silence in heaven for about half an hour.*

*8:3-4 And another angel came and stood at the altar with a golden censer, and he was given much incense to offer with the prayers of all the saints on the golden altar before the throne, and the smoke of the incense, with the prayers of the saints, rose before God from the hand of the angel.*

*8:5 Then the angel took the censer and filled it with fire from the altar and threw it on the earth, and there were peals of thunder, rumblings, flashes of lightning, and an earthquake.*

We see intensity increase from the 7th seal to the 7th trumpet as we notice past tense and present tense verbs amid God's wrath during the Day of the Lord.

Revelation 11:15-19 *Then the seventh angel blew his trumpet, and there were loud voices in heaven, saying, "The kingdom of the world has become the kingdom of our Lord and of his Christ, and he shall reign forever and ever." And the twenty-four elders who sit on their thrones before God fell on their faces and worshiped God, saying,*

> *"We give thanks to you, Lord God Almighty,*
> *who is and who was,*
> *for you have taken your great power*
> *and begun to reign.*
> *The nations raged,*
> *but your **wrath came**,*
> *and **the time** for the dead to be judged,*
> *and **for rewarding** your servants,*
> *the prophets and saints,*
> *and those who fear your name,*
> *both small and great,*
> *and **for destroying** the destroyers of the earth."*

*Then God's temple in heaven was opened, and the ark of his covenant was seen within his temple. There were flashes of lightning, rumblings, peals of thunder, an earthquake, and heavy hail.*

Finally, we see the last bowl at maximum intensity!

> Revelation 16:17-21 *The seventh angel poured out his bowl into the air, and a loud voice came out of the temple, from the throne, saying, "It is done!" And there were flashes of lightning, rumblings, peals of thunder, and a great earthquake such as there had never been since man was on the earth, so great was that earthquake. The great city was split into three parts, and the cities of the nations fell, and God remembered Babylon the great, to make her drain the cup of the wine of the fury of his wrath. And every island fled away, and no mountains were to be found. And great hailstones, about one hundred pounds each, fell from heaven on people; and they cursed God for the plague of the hail, because the plague was so severe.*

The 7th seal does not state any mention of hail. We see heavy hail during the 7th trumpet, then the worst hail of history during the 7th bowl. The earthquake is also most severe during the 7th bowl of wrath period. Events are intensified from the seal's opening to the execution of wrath.

There are not three sets of hail, or long periods between the seals, trumpets and bowls. Instead, the hail begins slowly, then ramps up.

This birth pang concept is also found in Isaiah 13:6-13 and Isaiah 26:16-21. Both passages are about the Day of the Lord where the Lord finally comes in full vengeance at the end of the age. The Lord also states raising the dead in Isaiah 26, so there are identical groupings from the Old Testament carrying over to the New Testament. In 2 Thessalonians 1:5-10 the unjust are punished and the just are rewarded at His coming like the O.T. examples.

## Sequencing Clues Determine the Order of End-Time Events

Again, contrary to what a casual reading might suggest, the sequence of events presented in Revelation is non-linear, or not set chronologically. There are overlaps in the seals, trumpets and bowls so that they do not follow each other. The 1st trumpet does not follow the 7th seal. For example, the 1st trumpet is placed during the 6th seal period.

The symbols used in Revelation can be traced to form an outline, but we also need other prophecies from the Old and New Testaments to complete the sequence of events. Here are some important chain links we will focus on.

**Scenes in Heaven** – The temple and throne room scenes gradually open as Heaven is finally revealed on earth.

**Day of the Lord** – This is the wrath of God being poured out upon the earth after the 6th seal is opened.

**Fire** – There are clues about fire symbols we will trace in relation to timing.

**Harvest** – The timing and symbols of the harvest in Revelation 14 have the same meanings as the parable of the Wheat and Tares in Matthew 13.

**Second Advent** – This is the most important event in Revelation and it shows that the chapters are non-linear.

**Resurrection of the Dead** – The symbol that depicts the resurrection at the rapture helps us understand overall timing.

**Time** – Timestamps are scattered throughout Revelation, especially the Great Tribulation Period.

## Scenes in Heaven Reveal the Sequence of Events

Don't miss statements clarifying that Heaven gradually "opens" as the scenes progress to reveal timing. The chapters are not in chronological order in relation to the scenes in Heaven. Here are three verses we will look at to follow the progression.

### Heaven Opening Passages

Revelation 11:19 *Then God's temple in **heaven** was **opened**, and the ark of his covenant was seen within his temple. There were flashes of lightning, rumblings, peals of thunder, an earthquake, and heavy hail.*

Revelation 15:5 *After this I looked, and the sanctuary of the tent of witness in **heaven** was **opened**,*

Revelation 19:11 *Then I saw **heaven opened**, and behold, a white horse! The one sitting on it is called Faithful and True, and in righteousness he judges and makes war.*

To understand these verses, we need to know the layout of the temple. Please refer to the original tabernacle design described in

Exodus 26 and Exodus 40, or temple images to learn how the gradual "opening" of Heaven can determine the sequence of events.

How do we know the order of events from these three passages in Revelation about Heaven opening? There are three scenes just like a movie that has flashbacks. We should notice that the tent of witness (tabernacle, temple) is opened in Revelation 15:5. This is the first event in the opening Heaven sequence, before the 7 bowls are poured out.

> Revelation 15:7-8 *And one of the four living creatures gave to the seven angels seven golden bowls full of the wrath of God who lives forever and ever, and the sanctuary was filled with smoke from the glory of God and from his power, and no one could enter the sanctuary until the seven plagues of the seven angels were finished.*

The key to finding the order of events is to notice that smoke is mentioned in verse 8. It is important to understand that no one will be able to go into or see inside the sanctuary of the temple until the wrath of God comes to completion. The smoke will fill the inner area of the temple immediately after it is opened.

The order of movement is from inside the temple to outside. The next event in this chain is the 7th trumpet that we notice in Revelation 11. The 7th trumpet will sound just before the second advent of Christ. The smoke is cleared after the angels pouring out the 7 bowls are finished with their work.

> Revelation 11:19 states that *"the ark of his covenant was seen within his temple."*

The ark will not be seen until the smoke clears, since it resides in the sanctuary. We can conclude that 7th bowl and the 7th trumpet are close in their timing. This concept also infers that Revelation is non-linear (i.e., the 1st bowl does not follow the 7th trumpet). The sanctuary does not open until the bowl judgments (Revelation 15:5), so it would be impossible to see the ark of the covenant if it is closed during the trumpets. The smoke clearing and the opening of the temple both help to identify the sequence of events.

The final scene of Heaven opening is found in Revelation 19:11. This is the second coming, the primary event that fits with all other passages about Heaven being completely open for the world to see Christ's advent. See Matthew 24:30-31 and Revelation 1:7. It is the timing of the merger of Heaven and earth (Ephesians 1:10, Revelation 21:2-3).

## Summary of Heaven Opening

1. The inner sanctuary of the temple opens prior to the 7 bowls.
2. The temple opens at the 7th trumpet.
3. Heaven completely opens at the second advent.

No spoilers, but later in our study, we'll examine sections that suggest scenes in Heaven previously unseen from earth will become visible at the second advent when Christ sets up His everlasting kingdom of Heaven on earth.

# The Day of the Lord Is the Wrath of God Poured Out

Statements referencing the Day of the Lord appear frequently throughout prophetic Scripture, so we can easily find it in Revelation by its references. It begins at the 6th seal, which is also during the Great Tribulation Period. The two periods overlap as we shall see later.

Please see Appendix 3 for a side-by-side comparison of Matthew 24 and the 7 seals. This table explains the transition from the beginning of birth pains found in seals 1 through 4, the beginning of the Great Tribulation Period in seal 5, and the beginning of the Day of the Lord in seal 6.

The 6th seal is opened in Revelation 6:12. John then reports a summary paraphrase by people of the earth in verse 17.

Revelation 6:15-17 *Then the kings of the earth and the great ones and the generals and the rich and the powerful, and everyone, slave and free, hid themselves in the caves and among the rocks of the mountains, calling to the mountains and rocks, "Fall on us and hide us from the face of him who is seated on the throne, and from the wrath of the Lamb, for* **the great day of their wrath has come***, and who can stand?"*

Isaiah 2 foresees the same concept of caves and rocks during the Day of the Lord. We do not need to believe in literal caves, although there is the possibility of this referring to the elite in their underground bunkers. The main point about hiding from God is that you cannot hide from God.

Verse 12

*For the **LORD of hosts has a day***
*against all that is proud and lofty,*
*against all that is lifted up—and it shall be brought low;*

*And people shall enter the caves of the rocks*
*and the holes of the ground,*
*from before the terror of the LORD,*
*and from the splendor of his majesty,*
*when he rises to terrify the earth.*

The same vision was shared with Isaiah and John. Isaiah also had other visions of the Day of the Lord that match Revelation. See Isaiah 13:6-13 and Isaiah 26:16-21.

The wrath of God will be completed around the time the 7th trumpet, when Armageddon occurs at the second advent. This passage puts the timing towards the end of the wrath period (bowls and trumpets).

Revelation 11:18

*The nations raged,*
*but **your wrath came,***
*and the **time for the dead to be judged,***
*and for rewarding your servants,*
*the prophets and saints,*
*and those who fear your name,*
*both small and great,*
*and **[time] for destroying***
***the destroyers of the earth.***

## Fire at the Time of Judgment

Fire is the cleansing term used to restore the earth at the time of judgment during the Day of the Lord. Peter said that the last days will be defined by fire.

> 2 Peter 3:7 *But by the same word the heavens and earth that now exist are stored up for fire, being kept until the day of judgment and destruction of the ungodly.*

We see fire mentioned several times in Revelation to help us place markers in the sequence of events.

*Revelation 8:3-5 And another **angel came and stood at the altar** with a golden censer, and he was given much incense to offer with the prayers of all the saints on the golden altar before the throne, and the smoke of the incense, with the prayers of the saints, rose before God from the hand of the angel. Then **the angel took the censer and filled it with fire from the altar and threw it on the earth**, and there were peals of thunder, rumblings, flashes of lightning, and an earthquake.*

Did you know that there is an angel in charge of fire? An easily overlooked detail, we see this same angel mentioned again in Revelation 14:15.

*And another **angel came out from the altar, the angel who has authority over the fire,** and he called with a loud voice to the one who had the sharp sickle, "Put in your sickle and gather the clusters from the vine of the earth, for its grapes are ripe."*

Do we think the angel will stand at the altar and wait six months for the trumpets to sound, then come out at the time of the bowl judgments? If you believe in a linear sequence of events, then the angel must wait a long time for the trumpets to be finished. However, the reading implies that the fire angel does his work at the 7th seal in Revelation 8, then comes out of the temple for the harvest at the second advent. This fits with our connecting passage concept that Revelation is non-linear.

There are many Day of the Lord events that occur between Revelation 8 and Revelation 14 that precede the 7th seal and the second advent. This is because John's visions move forward and backward in time, defying how we usually interpret things happening, so we cannot read Revelation and understand it without place markers.

There is another concept of fire regarding the sea of glass. In Revelation 4:6, we notice there is no fire on the sea of glass before the heavenly throne, but in Revelation 15 there is fire mixed in the sea. This fits with the timing of the second advent since fire is part of judgment on earth (2 Thessalonians 1:7-8).

> Revelation 15:2-3a *And I saw what appeared to be a* **sea of glass mingled with fire**—*and also those who had conquered the beast and its image and the number of its name, standing beside the sea of glass with harps of God in their hands. And they sing the song of Moses...*

This scene shifts to Heaven on earth at the second advent. In Revelation 4:6, the sea of glass is in the unseen realm of Heaven before the seals are opened. Heaven is revealed on earth at the second advent when the resurrection of the dead occurs. The fire on the sea of glass is fresh from the Day of the Lord. Finally, the resurrected will sing a new song on earth and the Song of Moses, which are both about judgement during the end times.

We know the timing of this because it is after tribulation that believers conquer the Mark of the Beast and because of the past tense verb used in Revelation 15:4b ... *for your righteous acts **have been revealed***.

## The Harvest Occurs at the Second Advent

One of the simplest analogies of the end times is the likeness to a harvest. Christ clearly explains this concept in the parable of the Wheat and Tares that mentions His coming.

Matthew 13:36-43 *Then he left the crowds and went into the house. And his disciples came to him, saying, "Explain to us the parable of the weeds of the field." He answered, "The one who sows the good seed is the Son of Man. The field is the world, and the good seed is the sons of the kingdom. The weeds are the sons of the evil one, and the enemy who sowed them is the devil. The harvest is the end of the age, and the reapers are angels. Just as the weeds are gathered and burned with fire, so will it be at the end of the age. The Son of Man will send his angels, and they will gather out of his kingdom all causes of sin and all law-breakers, and throw them into the fiery furnace. In that place there will be weeping and gnashing of teeth. Then the righteous will shine like the sun in the kingdom of their Father. He who has ears, let him hear.*

Here we see that the second advent is associated with angels and gathering the elect (rapture) while separating the unrighteous. This chain of events is reinforced in several passages such as Matthew 16:27, Matthew 24:29-31, Matthew 25:31-32, 1 Thessalonians 4:16, 2 Thessalonians 1:7-10, Jude 1:14-15, Revelation 19:11-21.

Revelation 14:14-19 *Then I looked, and behold, a white cloud, and seated on the cloud one like a son of man, with a golden crown on his head, and a sharp sickle in his hand. And another angel came out of the temple, calling with a loud voice to him who sat on the cloud, "Put in your sickle, and reap, for the hour to reap has come, for the harvest of the earth is fully ripe." So he who sat on the cloud swung his sickle across the earth, and the earth was reaped.*

*Then another angel came out of the temple in heaven, and he too had a sharp sickle. And another angel came out from the altar, the angel who has authority over the fire, and he called with a loud voice to the one who had the sharp sickle, "Put in your sickle and gather the clusters from the vine of the earth, for its grapes are ripe." So the angel swung his sickle across the earth and gathered the grape harvest of the earth and threw it into the great winepress of the wrath of God.*

The match between the harvest of Revelation and the parable of the Wheat and Tares is clear, since angels are always mentioned as part of the separation of believers and unbelievers. Angels are also mentioned to be a major part of the second advent. We will see in Chapter 24 that there are 10 passages about angels with Christ when He comes once more. Do we think there is separate rapture where Christ returns with angels then comes again after the Great Tribulation Period, or is the second coming and rapture one event identified with the same depictions?

## Second Advent Timing in Revelation

As previously seen in the Harvest passages, Revelation 14:14-19 and Revelation 19:11-16 clearly describe the second advent of Christ with angels gathering the elect and separating the wicked. Are there two second advents? Are there two different sets of angels harvesting? Of course not.

These seemingly contradictory statements referencing events that appear to happen at different times only further demonstrate that Revelation operates on a non-linear basis because major events are often repeated. There are also a lot of passages that are not in sequence in chapters 15 through 18, such as the Day of the Lord wrath judgments of the bowls supposedly occurring after Revelation 14. Revelation 14 should be considered as the same period of Revelation 19. The intermediate chapters 15 through 18 occur before the second advent, so Revelation 14 is out of place.

There is only one "winepress" in eschatology. The term is so specific that there cannot be a winepress at Armageddon and another at the second coming. There are not two great wars in a short span. The symbol of the winepress is used to correlate Revelation 14 and 19 with the timing of Christ's advent. See Isaiah 63:2-4, Revelation 14:19-20 and Revelation 19:15,

The 43rd chapter of Ezekiel states that the soles of the Lord's feet will touch down on earth, which is a very hard statement to use as a metaphor for spiritual feet. Ezekiel 43:7 is restated with the same feet mentioned in Zechariah 14:4, Acts 1:11, and Revelation 14:1. Another second advent term correlating Ezekiel 43 with Revelation is to consider the sound of "many waters." We can look to Ezekiel to see how his vision of the second advent is related.

> Ezekiel 43:2 *And behold, the glory of the God of Israel was coming from the east. And the sound of his coming was like the sound of* **many waters,** *and the earth shone with his glory.*

This phrase reinforces that Christ is shown to come to earth in chapters 14 and 19 of Revelation. We already have seen that the harvest and winepress concepts convey that these chapters are speaking of a single event, so this provides for an additional argument that Revelation is non-linear.

*Revelation 14:2 I heard a voice from heaven like the roar of **many waters** and like the sound of loud thunder*

*Revelation 19:6 I heard what seemed to be the voice of a great multitude, like the roar of **many waters** and like the sound of mighty peals of thunder*

## The Resurrection in the Book of Revelation

There is a very interesting visual from the Old Testament that we need to notice in Revelation. It is the depiction of the Lord and angels wearing bright clothes or white linen. We see this important concept carried over to Revelation. Remember that angels can look like men (Genesis 19), so sometimes prophets and apostles called them men.

**Passages About Bright Clothing Worn by the Righteous**

*Ezekiel 10:2 And he said to the man **clothed in linen**, "Go in among the whirling wheels underneath the cherubim. Fill your hands with burning coals from between the cherubim, and scatter them over the city." And he went in before my eyes.*

Daniel 7:9 *As I looked, thrones were placed, and the Ancient of Days took his seat; his **clothing was white** as snow, and the hair of his head like pure wool; his throne was fiery flames; its wheels were burning fire.*

Daniel 10:5 *I lifted up my eyes and looked, and behold, a man **clothed in linen**, with a belt of fine gold from Uphaz around his waist.*

Daniel 12:10 *Many shall purify themselves and make themselves **white** and be refined, but the wicked shall act wickedly. And none of the wicked shall understand, but those who are wise shall understand.*

Luke 24:4 *While they were perplexed about this, behold, two men stood by them in **dazzling apparel**.*

Revelation 3:4-5 *Yet you have still a few names in Sardis, people who have not soiled their garments, and they will walk with me in **white**, for they are worthy. The one who conquers will be clothed thus in **white garments**, and I will never blot his name out of the book of life. I will confess his name before my Father and before his angels.*

Revelation 3:18 *I counsel you to buy from me gold refined by fire, so that you may be rich, and **white garments** so that* *you may clothe yourself and the shame of your nakedness may not be seen, and salve to anoint your eyes, so that you may see.*

Revelation 4:4 *Around the throne were twenty-four thrones, and seated on the thrones were twenty-four elders, clothed in* **white garments**, *with golden crowns on their heads.*

Revelation 15:6 *and out of the sanctuary came the seven angels with the seven plagues, clothed in* **pure, bright linen,** *with golden sashes around their chests.*

Revelation 19:14 *And the armies of heaven, arrayed in* **fine linen, white and pure,** *were following him on white horses.*

It is interesting that Christ stated humans will be like angels after the resurrection. We can pursue this idea further to learn how it all fits together.

Luke 20:36 *for they cannot die anymore, because they are equal to angels and are sons of God, being sons of the resurrection.*

Now we arrive at the key resurrection timing passages in Revelation. We first notice that pure clothing is symbolically offered to martyrs under the altar at the 5th seal. This is the start of the Great Tribulation Period, before the second advent and resurrection. It is important to state that they are not yet wearing the robes, since they are souls without a body.

> Revelation 6:11 *Then they [martyrs] were each given a **white robe** and told to rest a little longer, until the number of their fellow servants and their brothers should be complete, who were to be killed as they themselves had been.*

Next, we see bright clothes are granted to be worn by the Bride of Christ (believers). This preparation occurs just before the second advent mentioned later in Revelation 19. Here, we can see that it is almost the time of the rapture (resurrection of the dead). The believers are still not wearing the robes in this verse, but it states the time to put them on.

<u>Revelation 19:8a</u>
*"it [the Bride] was granted her to clothe herself with fine linen, bright and pure"*

Finally, we notice white clothing being worn after the second advent. The resurrected believers are carrying palm branches, which signify the victory of Christ over the earth. This passage occurs on earth after the events of Revelation 19 (Armageddon).

> Revelation 7:9 *After this I looked, and behold, a great multitude that no one could number, from every nation, from all tribes and peoples and languages, standing before the throne and before the Lamb,* **clothed in white robes**, *with palm branches in their hands,*

These passages show a non-linear order of Revelation from Chapter 5 during the Great Tribulation Period, to Chapter 19 just before the resurrection, to Chapter 7 after the resurrection. The resurrection itself is not described like in 1 Corinthians 15:51-54 or 1 Thessalonians 4:15-17, but we know the general placement based upon the vast clothing imagery of the Bible. We can be assured that the saints wearing white clothing means they are granted an immortal body.

## Timing Mentioned in Revelation

Tour examination of how time is treated throughout Revelation continues with an investigation of phrases that reference when things should be happening or are supposed to happen. It is stated that time will stop counting at the end of the age during the 7th trumpet period as Christ comes to earth.

> Revelation 10:6-7 *[the angel] swore by him who lives forever and ever, who created heaven and what is in it, the earth and what is in it, and the sea and what is in it, that there would be **no more delay**, but that in the days of the trumpet call to be sounded by the seventh angel, the mystery of God would be fulfilled, just as he announced to his servants the prophets.*

The root word for "delay" is chronos – time. A better rendering is that there will be "no more time." The age of man will close, then the everlasting age of Christ's kingdom on earth will begin at His physical revelation for all the earth to see. The complete revelation of Christ is then fulfilled, unlike His first advent where He focused His work in Judea and surrounding areas.

We can also check the association of the 7th trumpet with the 7th bowl, since they are close in timing.

> Revelation 16:17 *The seventh angel poured out his bowl into the air, and a loud voice came out of the temple, from the throne, saying, "It is done!"*

There are no more judgments upon the earth as the Day of the Lord wrath period will be completed at the 7th bowl. This is the same period of the 7th seal when the final prayers of the saints are concluded in Revelation 8:4-5. Time will be no more, prayers will be closed, and there will be no more wrath upon the earth.

## The End of the Age

The concluding statement about prophetic completeness found in Revelation 10:5-7 that we examined previously does not mean all prophecies will be fulfilled at the 7th trumpet. The end of the age we live in will be complete. The mystery of God will be fulfilled as announced by the prophets of the O.T. Once these momentous events have come to pass, judgment and other prophetic realizations will occur during the next age.

The everlasting age begins when Christ establishes His throne on the restored earth, an unmistakable circumstance that will draw near once the signs become visible.

Daniel received a prophecy from an angel about the end of our age. The angel stated that people will understand the time of the end when it comes. Daniel 12 states:

Verse 4 *"But you, Daniel, shut up the words and seal the book, until the time of the end. Many shall run to and fro, and knowledge shall increase."*

Verse 9 *He said, "Go your way, Daniel, for the words are shut up and sealed until the time of the end."*

It is very interesting that a seal term is used by the angel. Are these the same seals that the lamb opens in the throne room of Revelation 6 and 8? Perhaps Christ has recently opened the first seal and the global empire of the 10 kingdoms are uniting towards the final beast system. If the next events are wars and famines of the second and third seals, we will know that the final countdown has begun.

# **Chapter 23**

## *What Is the Rapture?*

T he rapture is the transformation of our bodies to be like Christ's resurrected body. The everlasting nature of the rapture can be compared to our current condition. We will explore how we are spiritually risen with Christ today and how this differs from a physical resurrection in the future. The latter event is firmly placed during the second advent.

> <u>Philippians 3:20-21</u> *But our citizenship is in heaven, and from it we await a Savior, the Lord Jesus Christ, who will transform our lowly body to be like his glorious body, by the power that enables him even to subject all things to himself.*

Is this a physical transformation or spiritual? The entire faith of Christianity hinges upon a physical, bodily resurrection from death at the second advent. This is the foundation of the afterlife belief in the Bible. Paul makes this very clear in 1 Corinthians 15.

Verses 3-4 *For I delivered to you as of first importance what I also received: that Christ died for our sins in accordance with the Scriptures, that he was buried, that he was raised on the third day in accordance with the Scriptures,*

Verses 12-14 *Now if Christ is proclaimed as raised from the dead, how can some of you say that there is no resurrection of the dead? But if there is no resurrection of the dead, then not even Christ has been raised. And **if Christ has not been raised, then our preaching is in vain and your faith is in vain.***

Verses 17-19 *And **if Christ has not been raised, your faith is futile** and you are still in your sins. Then those also who have fallen asleep in Christ have perished. If in Christ we have hope in this life only, we are of all people most to be pitied.*

Verses 50-53 *Behold! I tell you a mystery. We shall not all sleep, but **we shall all be changed**, in a moment, in the twinkling of an eye, at the last trumpet. For the trumpet will sound, and **the dead will be raised imperishable**, and we shall be changed. For this perishable body must put on the imperishable, and **this mortal body must put on immortality**.*

There are cases we looked at in Chapter 7 about spiritual resurrections termed as "raising" or "lifting" types of root words that differ from the Greek word anastasis. Certainly, we are "raised" with Christ today in a spiritual sense, but this is not the entire gospel. There is the paradox that we are saved and not yet saved. Misunderstanding of the paradox has created problems of interpreting Revelation 20 that has split the Church into amillennial and premillennial beliefs of eschatology.

> Revelation 20:4... *I saw the souls of those who had been beheaded for the testimony of Jesus and for the word of God, and those who had not worshiped the beast or its image and had not received its mark on their foreheads or their hands.* **They came to life** *and reigned with Christ for a thousand years.*

Spiritualizing the first resurrection of Revelation 20:4 and Revelation 20:6 is an issue. If to "live again" means to be baptized or born again by the Spirit ("saved"), the people mentioned in the text must have been spiritually dead in their sins. The problem is that one group mentioned specifically was martyred (physical death is implied as martyrdom by beheading is a poor metaphor for spiritual death).

This brings up a conflict that the dead of Revelation 20 are physically dead but then resurrected to be spiritually alive under the amillennial view. This is not consistent use of literal or figurative language, even if a spirit only resurrection (not a bodily resurrection) is believed to be consciously reigning with Christ in His kingdom today. The viewpoint of the passage is on earth when they are resurrected. We should not utilize a hybrid mixing of literal and figurative language.

The text in Revelation 20 forces full mysticism or full bodily resurrection language, not a hybrid. Resurrections in the N.T. with a Greek anastasis root word meaning to "stand up" (such as John 11:23-24) are not used as spirit resurrections in other passages, so this would be the first usage. Revelation 20 would have stated other available Greek terms if a spiritual resurrection was intended.

2 Timothy 2:18 helps clarify bodily resurrection as a single future event from when Paul wrote his epistle. 1 John 3:2 also states that His appearing is in the future when we will be transformed. Prior to this, verse 1 John 2:28 correlates Christ's physical appearing with His coming (Parousia). The second coming (Parousia) and "appearing" are synonymous in second advent passages mentioned herein. The resurrection occurs when Christ physically comes again.

*Titus 2:11-13 For the grace of God has appeared, bringing salvation for all people, training us to renounce ungodliness and worldly passions, and to live self-controlled, upright, and godly lives in the present age, waiting for our blessed hope, the appearing of the glory of our great God and Savior Jesus Christ,*

Now we are saved based on the first advent stated in verse 11. We are not yet ultimately saved until the blessed hope mentioned in verse 13 comes at the second advent. The blessed hope is Christ's appearing, which is His physical return in the future tense. Seen with eyes = second advent = Parousia.

The implications here draw us into an inescapable paradox. Now we are saved, and we are not yet saved. We need to understand this "now and not yet" concept if we are to understand the rapture. People have trouble with paradoxes, but the Bible has its share of them. Salvation is another example that God uses paradoxes throughout scripture. There are many passages that suggest a physical salvation message of the resurrection, others speak to spiritual salvation, and thankfully some speak of both to make it clearer.

Bodily resurrection language at His coming to this realm where eyes can see His return (as in Matthew 24:30) is throughout scripture such as Job 19:25-27. "Appearing" is used in the future tense in second advent passages mentioned in 2 Thessalonians 2:8, 2 Timothy 4:8, Titus 2:13, Hebrews 9:28, 1 Peter 5:4, 1 John 3:2 and Colossians 3 also states what happens when Christ appears.

> Colossians 3:1-4 *"If then you have been **raised** with Christ, seek the things that are above, where Christ is, seated at the right hand of God. Set your minds on things that are above, not on things that are on earth. For you have died, and your life is hidden with Christ in God. **When Christ** who is your life **appears, then you** also **will appear with him in glory**."* (v.6 also has a Day of the Lord reference)

Paul explains the paradox in Colossians when he used figurative language of the metaphor "raised" in the past tense, but it describes an actual event that took place when the believer was baptized / born again. Being raised with Christ references a spiritual lifting event (the second birth mentioned by Christ to Nicodemus in John 3:3-7). The passage then moves on to the appearing (second coming) in the future tense. Appendix 2 has more information about the verb tenses of salvation.

# Is the Rapture Before, During or After the Great Tribulation Period?

Why bother with the warnings from Daniel, Christ, Paul, and John if the Holy Spirit is the restrainer, and the Church is absent during the Great Tribulation period when the antichrist will be revealed? There are clear warnings not to take the mark of the beast, so this would not really be necessary to warn unbelievers only. Not to mention that there are believers who go into captivity during this period and those who are killed for not taking the mark of the beast, because these are specially mentioned and rewarded in Revelation 20:4 to enter the kingdom's reign period.

A pretribulation rapture is only possible within the interpretation of 2 Thessalonians 2:7 if the Holy Spirit is the restrainer. If the Holy Spirit is not the restrainer mentioned, then the pretribulation rapture theory falls apart completely. We also need to remember that ultimate salvation is granted at the second advent, since we are not "completely saved" now or in the past tense. We are sealed (Ephesians 1:13-14) for the future to be spared from God's wrath and finally granted eternal life at the second advent.

The texts are devoid of passages, suggesting that the Holy Spirit leaves the Church on earth or that He is taking the Church to Heaven during tribulation in any Scripture. In fact, we find ample evidence for the opposite. Christ will be with us always until the end of the age. Matthew 24:3 and Matthew 28:20 correlate to the second coming at the end of Daniel's 70th week (the time of the Gentiles cannot be confused with the time clock of the promised land to be fulfilled as the everlasting kingdom being establish in the next age).

The Church (Messianic Jews and Gentiles) goes through the Great Tribulation as does Israel of blood descent. There would be no need for warnings to the 7 Churches (including us today) not to take the mark of the beast, or that we may die by the sword or go into captivity. Revelation 13:9-10 is clear that this is written for the saints because the context of Chapter 13 depicts believers on earth during the Great Tribulation Period with the Mark of the Beast being mentioned.

Now we are ready to see how the Day of the Lord relates to the rapture and the Great Tribulation Period. Paul explains the relationships in 2 Thessalonians.

2 Thessalonians 1:7-10 *and to grant relief to you who are afflicted as well as to us, when the Lord Jesus is revealed from heaven with his mighty angels in flaming fire, inflicting vengeance on those who do not know God and on those who do not obey the gospel of our Lord Jesus. They will suffer the punishment of eternal destruction, away from the presence of the Lord and from the glory of his might, when he comes on that day to be glorified in his saints, and to be marveled at among all who have believed, because our testimony to you was believed.*

2 Thessalonians 2:1-3 *Now concerning the coming of our Lord Jesus Christ and our being gathered together to him, we ask you, brothers, not to be quickly shaken in mind or alarmed, either by a spirit or a spoken word, or a letter seeming to be from us, to the effect that the day of the Lord has come. Let no one deceive you in any way. For that day will not come, unless the rebellion comes first, and the man of lawlessness is revealed, the son of destruction,*

## 2 Thessalonians Summary

- The Day of the Lord will not arrive until after the antichrist is revealed.
- Christ's next advent is associated with the Day of the Lord.
- The rapture is not realized until Christ comes.

**Summary** – the antichrist must be revealed before the Day of the Lord, which means that the rapture occurs after the Great Tribulation Period begins, at some point during the Day of the Lord.

We can't overlook another glaring problem for a pre-tribulation rapture, the mention of "the Day of the Lord." It must be completely disassociated from the coming of Christ in <u>verse 1</u> of 2 Thessalonians 2 if a pre-trib rapture is correct, yet Paul associates all three milestones in succession.

2 Thessalonians 1 states the "revealing" in verse 7 and His "coming" in verse 10. The context is clear for Chapter 2 to be based upon Chapter 1 using synonyms for the second advent that the Day of the Lord is always associated with.

Why wouldn't Paul have made it crystal clear if there was a pre-tribulation rapture? This is because he was referencing Daniel, so there was no need to make it any clearer. He already taught the Church of

Thessalonica in person. He was reminding them of his teaching based upon Daniel about the man of sin (Daniel called the "little horn" but is the same person as the antichrist where Paul called him the "man of lawlessness").

If the Day of the Lord in verses 2-3 of 2 Thessalonians 2 is the same time period as the coming of the Lord in verse 1, then the pre-trib rapture theory falls apart completely. It seems obvious that Paul is speaking of the same day simply by reading the text alone with no preconceived idea of a pre-trib rapture. However, preconceived notions yield forced interpretation over clear wording.

The "Day of the Lord" is a well-known term. Matthew 24:29 is the same event as in Joel 2:1-2, 10-11, 30-32, and Joel 3:12-16 which defines most of the Day of the Lord language. It comes at the end of the Great Tribulation and is the time when Christ comes at the second advent presented in Matthew 24:29-30. The main point is that Christ speaks to this event occurring after the Great Tribulation and Paul repeats this same concept with the man of sin being revealed before the Day of the Lord (before the second coming).

## Day of the Lord Timing

The second advent is at the end Day of the Lord timing – 2 Thessalonians 2:1 = 2 Thessalonians 2:2-3

Another passage to verify is <u>Isaiah 24:21-23</u>. This passage is at the end of the Day of the Lord where satan is locked in the pit. This will occur when Christ comes again in Revelation 19 then has an angel lock him into the pit afterward in <u>Revelation 20:1-3</u>. These passages are identical in that evil ones are locked up for a while, then punished later after their release. We see clear parallels of Isaiah 24:21-23 with Revelation 20.

Isaiah, Joel and Christ state signs of the sun, moon, and stars that occur after the Great Tribulation right before the timing of the second coming. He comes after the 6th seal in <u>Revelation 6:12-13</u>. The same signs of the Day of the Lord are mentioned in the 6th seal.

Paul states that the antichrist will be revealed before this Day of the Lord that includes all these heavenly signs. The Great Tribulation period is at the time of the antichrist, so Paul stated that our gathering with Christ is after the antichrist is revealed. This means that a post-tribulation rapture event should be considered as anything else is not possible in this text of 2 Thessalonians 2.

The book of Revelation has more to say about "revealing."

First, let's look at other N.T. passages speaking to the revelation of Christ in the future (<u>Luke 17:30</u>).

Romans 2:5 *"But because of your hard and impenitent heart you are storing up wrath for yourself on the **day of wrath** when God's righteous judgment **will be revealed**."*

Romans 8:18-19 *"For I consider that the sufferings of this present time are not worth comparing with the glory that is **to be revealed** to us. For the creation waits with eager longing for the **revealing** of the sons of God."*

1 Corinthians 1:7 *"so that you are not lacking in any gift, as you **wait for the revealing** of our Lord Jesus Christ,"*

1 Corinthians 3:13 *"each one's work will become manifest, for **the Day** will disclose it, because it **will be revealed** by fire, and the fire will test what sort of work each one has done."*

Philippians 3:10-21 has a future tense meaning about the second advent and resurrection throughout this extensive passage to consider.

2 Thessalonians 1:7 *"and to grant relief to you who are afflicted as well as to us, **when the Lord Jesus is revealed** from heaven with his mighty angels"*

This revelation mentioned in 2 Thessalonians Chapter 1 is a widely used term that is mentioned before the Day of the Lord text in Chapter 2 of Paul's second epistle to the Church at Thessalonica. The associated meaning of "revealed" to "gathering" to "coming" to "appearing" to "Day of the Lord" is speaking of the same second advent. With this background, we can now shift gears to his most famous rapture passage.

> 1 Thessalonians 4:13-17 *"But we do not want you to be uninformed, brothers, about those who are asleep [those who died], that you may not grieve as others do who have no hope. For since we believe that Jesus died and rose again, even so, through Jesus, God will bring [their spirit] with him those who have fallen asleep. For this we declare to you by a word from the Lord, that we who are alive, who are left until the coming of the Lord, will not precede those who have fallen asleep. For the Lord himself will descend from heaven with a cry of command, with the voice of an archangel, and with the sound of the trumpet of God. And the dead in Christ will rise first [spirits enter back into the physical realm]. Then we who are alive, who are left, will be* **caught up** *[raptured – snatched or grabbed out of harm's way] together with them in the clouds to meet the Lord in the air, and so we will always be with the Lord."*

Those who are alive at His coming will be raptured (1 Thessalonians 4:17). Rapture simply means to snatch (or save) from destruction coming upon the earth. It is not associated with the feeling people have when they are in some hypnotic state.

Here is another example of snatching found in Jude 1:22-23 using the same root word as the rapture. To be snatched means saved from wrath in this context, so Paul and Jude utilized the same concept. The wicked are destroyed (taken away) and the just are saved (kept, left to be with Christ) from destruction.

Luke 17:33-37 has an opposite meaning of what adherents believe happens in a pre-tribulation rapture. This was briefly described in Chapter 6. Luke 17 explains who are taken to the vultures (the wicked) and who are left to be with Christ. The Biblical texts show that the saved (raptured) are kept with Christ to enter Heaven on earth. Matthew 13's parable of the Wheat and Tares depicts this concept (Matthew 13:36-43). The wheat is kept while the tares are taken away (burned). The rapture event is not being "taken" to Heaven. Instead, we are kept (saved) from harm's way.

One of our primary goals is to organize all second coming passages into a consistent theoretical framework based on common themes. They can fit if we allow the passages to work in conjunction, since some passages like Matthew 24:40-41 don't describe all the details about who is taken and who is left on earth when Christ comes again. Luke 17:33-37 is very similar to Matthew 24:40-41, yet Luke adds the additional statement about the people who are "taken" as going to the vultures.

*Luke 17:33-37 "Whoever seeks to preserve his life will lose it, but whoever loses his life will keep it. I tell you, in that night there will be two in one bed. One will be taken and the other left. There will be two women grinding together. One will be taken and the other left." And they said to him, "Where, Lord?" He said to them, "Where the corpse is, there the vultures will gather."*

The Days of Noah is also a good analogy of timing before the wrath of God is poured out again upon the earth, since both Peter and Christ use the flood to explain their point.

*Matthew 24:38-39 "For as in those days before the flood they were eating and drinking, marrying and giving in marriage, until the day when Noah entered the ark, and they were unaware until the flood came and swept them all away, so will be the coming of the Son of Man"*

The key phrase that stands out and demands attention here is "swept away" to mean they were taken away just like weeds in the harvest parable. The root word means to "take up" or "lift," so again we see "taken" being ascribed to the wicked people.

Christ is more specific in Luke. "Destroyed" is used instead of taken or swept away.

> Luke 17:26-27 *"Just as it was in the days of Noah, so will it be in the days of the Son of Man. They were eating and drinking and marrying and being given in marriage, until the day when Noah entered the ark, and the flood came and destroyed them all."*

In 2 Peter 2:5, we see Noah as preserved, kept, spared, etc., from the impending judgment of the flood. This is our example. Noah went through the flood but was spared the judgment of the flood (i.e., spared God's wrath).

It shouldn't escape anyone's knowledge that believers and unbelievers will continue to live and co-exist together on earth until the second advent. The important knowledge to grasp right now is that believers will be in the "ark" with Christ during the wrath period. In the case of the final outpouring, we will be in the "clouds" according to Paul, not an ark.

## All Eyes Will See Christ's Return

Uses of related "optic" and "epiphany" root words convey physical eyes involved to see Him when He arrives. Passages such as Matthew 24:30, Luke 17:24, Luke 17:30 and Revelation 1:7 convey a physical appearance of Christ. All end-time events revolve around a physical second advent and resurrection that everyone will see. We do not want to over-spiritualize Revelation (even though it is filled with symbols and metaphors).

Advent = "appearing." Appearing has the same meaning of royalty arriving ("Parousia" in Greek) as correlated in 1 John 2:28. Christ's "coming" translated into English means a royal appearance. The second advent is a royal event where all eyes will see.

Considering all passages, "appearing" can be understood such as the term used after His resurrection (see Luke 24:34 and Acts 1:3). Taken out of context, some may think Revelation depicts symbolic or metaphorical appearances that mean something besides physical. Revelation 14:14 and 19:11 both have symbolic language, but they are associated to other events with clear language that are literally optical.

Now we can better see how the second advent and rapture are intimately connected with the Day of the Lord and the Great

Tribulation Period. Next, we will examine more passages about the association of all these important events to verify they are consistent.

# Chapter 24

## Does the Rapture Occur at the Second Advent?

T wo of the most discussed biblical events are the rapture and the second advent. But how else do they relate to one another, and can we be sure they take place at the same time? Let's explore the Old Testament and New Testament prophecies predicting the concurrence of the rapture with the second advent of Christ. The goal will be to achieve a time sequence understanding of the resurrection of the dead and events mentioned in the tribulation and wrath periods. Thirty-six different second advent passages will be examined with a focus on aligning repeated themes and elements to obtain the prize that awaits completion of this study.

"Rapture" and "resurrection" at the second coming are related terms since the resurrection of the dead occurs at the rapture. However, rapture has a broader meaning. Rapture means to be "snatched" in salvation terms within eschatology (i.e., "grabbed" by Christ to be saved from fire or death). There is no event found in the biblical text where salvation of living saints on earth at Christ's coming is separated in time from salvation of departed saints.

Rapture will be the preferred term to include the transformation of the living (Philippians 3:20-21) and the resurrection of the dead (1 Corinthians 15:51-53). Ultimate salvation occurs at the rapture. It means eternal life in a new body.

A "post-trib" rapture also means that salvation occurs at the second advent, except it's associated with the end of the 3.5-year Great Tribulation Period mentioned in Daniel and Revelation. It is fulfillment of being saved today – 2 Corinthians 5:1-5, Ephesians 1:13-14.

An "end-wrath" rapture is like a post-trib rapture other than that it is confined to the second advent and rapture starting at the 7th trumpet of Revelation 11. This rapture is during the 7th bowl period (Revelation 16:17-21), slightly after the 7th trumpet sounds. This does not mean that the saints living on earth realize God's wrath directly (Romans 2:5-10, Romans 5:9, 1 Thessalonians 1:10, 1 Thessalonians 5:9), but that they will be protected by being grabbed out of harm's way (saved) until this wrath is completely poured out. The symbolic 144,000 of Revelation 14:1 are also spared from God's wrath while on earth.

A way to describe similarities between post-trib and end-wrath raptures is to coin a new phrase I hope you'll find useful. Let's call it a "wrath-avoiding" rapture. Both views could utilize the same definition where the second coming is an extended event that occurs at the end of the tribulation period, and it takes a little time to complete during the end of the wrath period (vs. an "instantaneous" second coming). Keep this in mind as we look at the reasons behind why this makes sense.

## Key Relationships to the Second Advent

This brings us to relational elements. We can better understand the second advent when it is linked with the rapture and other events of this period. We will have a better appreciation for the last days upon closer examination of 36 passages that have integrated elements as part of one major series of rapid events.

### Combined Elements During the 2nd Coming

**Second Advent** – This the primary event that drives everything else. It is explicitly mentioned in most of the 36 passages referenced in this chapter. It is sometimes implied if there is enough related evidence to qualify as an indirect reference.

**Rapture** – This previously defined term is not always mentioned in the 36 second advent passages, but is included in 39% of them. The word "rapture" in English is never used since this is derived from an old Latin root word. However, we will use "rapture" when salvation passages are mentioned adjacent to the second coming (rapture = transformation of the living or resurrection of the dead when Christ appears next time).

**Judgment** – There are a few types of judgment that occur at the second advent. The judgment of the just and the judgment of the unjust as individuals are described in most cases, but destructive judgment upon groups is also stated.

**Physical Appearance** – These passages describe a bodily return of Christ to earth that will be witnessed by people's eyes. This is a physical rendering, not spiritual or figurative eyesight. Examples of the first advent (Luke 24:34, Acts 1:3) are like the second.

**Clouds** – The glory of the Lord described in the Old Testament (Exodus 16:10) is magnified in the New Testament by depicting Christ's return in glory on, in and with clouds. Literal and figurative uses of the term can be examined in 7 of the 36 passages that state "clouds" at the second advent.

**Angels or Armies** – There are five passages that describe a warlike group of angels that accompany Christ upon His return to earth.

**Angels Gathering or Separating** – There are five other passages that describe angels, not as warlike but as gathering the saints or separating the wicked. This totals 10 of 36 passages that depict angels coming with Christ in two distinct ways.

**Voice or Command** – Christ will speak audibly at His return. In all cases, His voice initiates the rapture, to transform the living or resurrect the dead. This was foreshadowed by the resurrection of Lazarus where Christ spoke towards his tomb (John 11:43).

**Trumpet** – Sometimes there is a trumpet sound mentioned at the second advent.

**Tribulation** – Several passages state Christ's return after a tribulation period. There is not one passage in the Bible that states any secretive or physical appearance of Christ before tribulation. He always comes at the end. Spiritual appearances of Christ into a person's heart are not in an eschatological context, so these passages are not considered as end-time related.

**Destruction of the Wicked** – 16 of 36 passages state that Christ (or angels with Christ) repays the unjust for their wicked deeds. Some passages state salvation for the just and punishment for the unjust during the same period of His recompense when He arrives.

Click here to download a PDF file comprising an organized table of these passages, or copy this link in a browser –

kjsoze.com/daniel-and-revelation-passages/

## Passages of the Second Coming of Christ

All passages with a direct reference to the second coming are listed below throughout each section. Only 1 passage does not reference the second coming, Daniel 12. However, this is an important chapter that includes other elements such as the resurrection and judgment. We know from Daniel 7 that Christ comes to earth, so the book of Daniel has known references. Daniel 12 is included in our list to help show more relationships to the 3.5-year tribulation period laid out by Daniel (repeated in Revelation).

Passages that have implied references to the second coming are – Daniel 2:31-45, Matthew 13:36-43, John 6:39-40, Revelation 11:15-18, Revelation 17:14.

## Passages of the Rapture

Job 19:25-27, Isaiah 26:19-21, Daniel 12, John 5:21-29, John 6:39-40, 1 Corinthians 15:12-28, 1 Corinthians 15:50-53, 1 Thessalonians 3:13 (implied), 1 Thessalonians 4:13-17, Philippians 3:10-21, Hebrews 9:27-28 (implied), 1 Peter 1:3-9, 1 John 2:28-3:2 (implied), Revelation 11:15-18 (implied)

## Passages About Judgment for the Just

Daniel 7:9-27, Daniel 12 (implied), Matthew 13:36-43, Matthew 16:27, Matthew 25:31-46, John 5:21-29, 1 Corinthians 4:5, 1 Thessalonians 3:13, 2 Thessalonians 1:5-10, 1 Timothy 6:13-16 (implied), 2 Timothy 4:1-8, Philippians 3:10-21, Hebrews 9:27-28, 1 Peter 1:3-9, 1 Peter 5:4, Revelation 11:15-18, Revelation 22:12

## Passages About Judgment Against the Unjust

Daniel 7:9-27, Daniel 12 (implied), Matthew 13:36-43, Matthew 16:27, Matthew 25:31-46, John 5:21-29, 2 Thessalonians 1:5-10, 2 Thessalonians 2:1-12, Jude 1:14-15, Revelation 19:11-21, Revelation 22:12

## Passages of the Physical Appearance of Christ

Job 19:25-27, Matthew 24:15-31, Luke 17:22-37, Luke 21:25-28, 1 John 2:28-3:2, Revelation 1:7

## Passages with Clouds Depicted at Christ's Return

Daniel 7:9-27, Matthew 24:15-31, Luke 21:25-28, Acts 1:9-11, 1 Thessalonians 4:13-17, Revelation 1:7, Revelation 14:14-20

## Passages with Angels / Armies Accompanying Christ

Matthew 16:27, 1 Thessalonians 4:13-17, 2 Thessalonians 1:5-10, Jude 1:14-15, Revelation 19:11-21

## Passages with Angels Gathering the Righteous Saints or Separating the Unjust

Matthew 13:36-43, Matthew 24:15-31, Matthew 25:31-46, 2 Thessalonians 2:1-12 (implied), Revelation 14:14-20

## Passages with Christ's Command to Initiate the Rapture

John 5:21-29, 1 Thessalonians 4:13-17, Philippians 3:10-21

## Passages with a Trumpet at the Rapture, or a Trumpet at Judgment Day

Matthew 24:15-31, 1 Corinthians 15:50-53, 1 Thessalonians 4:13-17, Revelation 11:15-18 (also states that this trumpet sounds the beginning of Christ's reign on earth)

## Passages about Christ Arriving after Tribulation

Daniel 7:9-27, Daniel 12, Matthew 24:15-31, Luke 21:25-28 (implied), 2 Thessalonians 2:1-12, Revelation 17:14, Revelation 19:11-21 (Revelation passages implied)

## Passages about Destruction of the Wicked at the Second Coming

Isaiah 26:19-21, Daniel 2:31-45, Daniel 7:9-27, Daniel 12, Matthew 13:36-43, Matthew 25:31-46, Luke 17:22-37, 1 Corinthians 15:12-28, 2 Thessalonians 1:5-10, 2 Thessalonians 2:1-12, Philippians 3:10-21, Jude 1:14-15, Revelation 11:15-18, Revelation 14:14-20, Revelation 17:14, Revelation 19:11-21

## Bible Passages About the Second Coming

All 36 of these passages connect to each other by sharing eleven parts of the ending chapter of history. There is no passage referenced that states Christ will come again without using at least one of the other eleven associations. For example, He comes "with His angels" or He comes "to judge." Related elements show up from 8% to 45% of these 36 second advent passages.

Three is the lowest number of second advent characteristics that are repeated (8%). This is Christ's voice at His coming (mentioned 3 times out of 36 passages).

The highest numbers are the rapture at 14, destruction of the wicked at 16 and a positive judgment in favor of the just at 17 of 36 passages.

In statistics, there are compounding relationship to relationship formulas that make the likelihood of a single sequence of end-time events the logical conclusion. It is nearly impossible that there are two separate destructions of the wicked or two separate reward judgments at two separate advents of Christ. A tough challenge for the pre-trib rapture view is to explain an initial resurrection at this rapture, then a different resurrection event at the second coming. No text supports this.

This is not a chapter about math, so we will look at base logic. For example, in 1 Corinthians 4:5 there is the second advent depicted with judgment in favor of the saints. It is specifically stated that this reward judgment occurs after He comes.

> *Therefore do not pronounce judgment before the time, before* **the Lord comes,** *who will bring to light the things now hidden in darkness and will disclose the purposes of the heart.* **Then each one will receive his commendation** *from God.*

While angels are not mentioned in 1 Corinthians 4:5, we should not overlook that they are associated near the time of rewards for the righteous in other passages. In Matthew 16:27 the second advent is described with judgment and with an accompaniment of angels.

> *For the Son of Man is going to **come with his** **angels** in the glory of his Father, and **then he** **will repay** each person according to what he has done.*

We also see angels again in 2 Thessalonians 1:5-8, this time with more action on the angels' part.

> *This is evidence of the righteous judgment of God, that you may be considered worthy of the kingdom of God, for which you are also suffering— since indeed God considers it just to repay with affliction those who afflict you, and to grant relief to you who are afflicted as well as to us, **when the Lord Jesus is revealed** from heaven **with his mighty angels in flaming fire, inflicting vengeance** on those who do not know God and on those who do not obey the gospel of our Lord Jesus.*

There are differences in Christ coming with or without angels. We also see outright statements arguing the second coming is a good thing for saints but a bad thing for the unrighteous. Are they discrete events or different angels?

The next two verses in 2 Thessalonians 1:9-10 make the case for a single event even clearer.

> *They will suffer the punishment of eternal destruction, away from the presence of the Lord and from the glory of his might,* **when he comes on that day to be glorified in his saints,** *and to be marveled at among all who have believed, because our testimony to you was believed.*

Here we see in 2 Thessalonians 1 that the wicked are punished, and that there is relief for the saints at the same time of Christ's glorification ("that day"). In these passages, we notice accompanying angels and judgment in relation to each other within the entire biblical context, even if a passage such as 1 Corinthians 4:5 does not specifically state something like angels. This same grouping concept is magnified over 36 passages.

The other option we face is that there are at least two accompaniments of angels, two uses of trumpets, etc., until there is a force of multiple returns of Christ. This is a paramount question to answer. Is Christ coming back once or more than once? Let's stick with Hebrews 9:27-28.

*And just as it is appointed for man to die once, and after that comes judgment, so Christ, having been offered once to bear the sins of many, **will appear a second time**, not to deal with sin but to save those who are eagerly waiting for him.*

To honor the words of Hebrews 9:28, some who believe in a pre-trib rapture feel that Christ does not physically, technically, come back to earth within this rapture view. He hangs out in the "air" so a belief in only one second coming to earth holds true. However, since the signs or elements of a pre-trib rapture may be shared between other passages, adherents need to explain two sets of angels, two different trumpets, etc. Logic (or math) does not lead us to a conclusion of two or more of any elements or two second advents.

Some of these passages identified only state one or two sub-events within the second advent. Christ coming to earth is the major thrust where something like a voice command or trumpet sound is just a small part of the overall episode. It is more revealing with passages like Daniel 7, Matthew 24 and 1 Thessalonians 4 that include several parts of the whole.

> 1 Thessalonians 4:13-17 *But we do not want you to be uninformed, brothers, about those who are asleep, that you may not grieve as others do who have no hope. For since we believe that Jesus died and rose again, even so, through Jesus, God will bring with him those who have fallen asleep. For this we declare to you by a word from the Lord, that we who are alive, who are left until the **coming of the Lord**, will not precede those who have fallen asleep. For the Lord himself will descend from heaven with a **cry of command**, with the voice of an **archangel**, and with the **sound of the trumpet** of God. And the **dead in Christ will rise** first. Then we who are alive, who are left, will be **caught up** [snatched] together with them in the **clouds** to meet the Lord in the air, and so we will always be with the Lord.*

This interesting description of the second advent gives the mind plenty of grist for thought, including Christ's command, an archangel, a trumpet, clouds, and the resurrection of the dead along with the salvation of living saints at the rapture. This is 6 out of 11 aspects that are associated with each other. Daniel 7 also has 6 of the 11 aspects.

Matthew 24:29-31 is another famous passage that contains several second advent elements (6 of 11).

> ***Immediately after the tribulation*** *of those days the sun will be darkened, and the moon will not give its light, and the stars will fall from heaven, and the powers of the heavens will be shaken. Then will appear in heaven the sign of the Son of Man, and then all the tribes of the earth will mourn, and **they will see** the **Son of Man coming** on the **clouds** of heaven with power and great glory. And he will send out his **angels** with a loud **trumpet** call, and they will gather his elect from the four winds, from one end of heaven to the other.*

Once we realize that there is only one set of clouds, one trumpet and one of everything else, we can be reassured of end-time sequencing. In Matthew 24, Christ states He will come after the Day of the Lord signs that are "immediately after the tribulation." This is further corroborated by 2 Thessalonians 2:1-12. Paul explains that history's greatest antichrist will be revealed before Christ comes again (at the time when the saints are gathered).

This future antichrist is active during the Great Tribulation Period. Christ comes after this tribulation at the time of the destruction of the antichrist and the rest of the wicked (another common theme with 16 out of 36 passages stating the same concept of destruction of the wicked).

## Determining the Sequence of End-Time Events

We can assemble an order of events now that we have examined several passages. The primary goal for timing is to answer the question about the timing sequence related to the second coming. Since an alignment of key phrases is prevalent, and there does not seem to be any reason to believe in a third appearing of Christ, it is reasonable that there is the following high-level order.

**Antichrist** is revealed before the Day of the Lord (2 Thessalonians 2:1-3) – the Great Tribulation Period leads to wars and troubles for the saints as shown in Daniel 7:25-26, Revelation 12:17, Revelation 17:14 and these similar passages:

Daniel 7:21-22b *As I looked, this horn [antichrist]* **made war with the saints** *and prevailed over them, until the Ancient of Days came...*

Revelation 13:7-8 *Also it [beast / antichrist] was allowed to* **make war on the saints** *and to conquer them. And authority was given it over every tribe and people and language and nation, and all who dwell on earth will worship it, everyone whose name has not been written before the foundation of the world in the book of life of the Lamb who was slain.*

**Armageddon** – The last battle of this age assembles at the 6th trumpet and 6th bowl periods of Revelation 9:13-20 and Revelation 16:12-16. The 6th seal is opened prior to the assembly to allow the Day of the Lord events with wrath pouring out on the wicked. We see Isaiah 13:4-13 and Joel 3:11-16 referencing the same 6th seal signs and the gathering of nations against the Lord. Armageddon is associated with the Day of the Lord.

**Christ's Advent** – There are many sub-events that occur within this same period.

The everlasting (millennial) kingdom reign begins on earth – Revelation 11:17 and Revelation 20:4.

**Rapture** – the righteous are saved from impending doom – 1 Thessalonians 1:10, 1 Thessalonians 5:1-10. There is no verse combining the rapture with the second advent in Revelation, but Revelation 17:14 points to the saints already being with Christ when destruction of the wicked occurs at the final battle. It is safe to assume that the rapture of Revelation 20:4 has already occurred in Revelation 17's reference to the end of Armageddon.

Wrath is completely poured out (7th bowl – Revelation 16:17-21 with Revelation 11:18 stating the end of wrath's completion) Tribulation and wrath are finished.

**Judgment of individuals** – Revelation 11:18, Revelation 20:4. We know from many passages this occurs after His return to earth (Matthew 25:31-32).

## Post-Trib or End-Wrath Rapture?

Even though we have assembled an outline of high-level events, we still have not concluded if a post-trib or end-wrath rapture is a better term to use. Tribulation and wrath will be defined more below before we answer.

Tribulation is a broad term. It has been occurring for thousands of years (John 16:33, Acts 14:22, Romans 8:35, Romans 12:12). None of these references state "great" tribulation.

We can't be so caught up in trying to ascribe meaning that we confuse the Great Tribulation Period with general tribulation. When we're looking for passages relating to the Great Tribulation Period, we find a key one in Matthew 24:21.

> For then there will be **great tribulation**, such as has not been from the beginning of the world until now, no, and never will be.

Great Tribulation is the same as the 3.5-year period mentioned in Daniel and Revelation (Daniel 7:25, Daniel 12:7, Revelation 13:5).

The hard part is matching the Great Tribulation Period with wrath timing because they overlap at the Day of the Lord. However, it is easier to align everything if we focus our attention on "wrath." Here are some wrath passages about age-ending judgments.

> Romans 2:5 *But because of your hard and impenitent heart you are storing up wrath for yourself on the* **day of wrath** *when God's righteous judgment* **will be revealed**. The "day" of wrath does not necessarily refer to a single day of 24 hours.

> Revelation 6:17a *for the great day of their* **wrath has come**, *and who can stand?* The 6th seal points to the Day of the Lord at the beginning of the wrath period.

> Revelation 11:18a *The nations raged, but your* **wrath came**. This 7th trumpet section provides a lot of details about timing. It does not state wrath or destruction of the wicked is complete. It does state it is time for "destroying the destroyers." Revelation 11:17-18 also states the time is at hand for judgment of the dead and Christ's reign beginning on earth. This brief passage is another cluster of related events. Wrath begins earlier, so the 7th trumpet must be just before the last bowl judgment, when destruction is complete.

*Revelation 14:19 So the angel swung his sickle across the earth and gathered the grape harvest of the earth and threw it into the great winepress of the **wrath** of God.* This section repeats Old Testament winepress passages such as Isaiah 63:1-6 and Joel 3:11-16. Revelation 14 is a parallel passage to Revelation 19:19-21 when wrath is completed.

*Revelation 15:1 Then I saw another sign in heaven, great and amazing, seven angels with seven plagues, which are the last, for with them the **wrath of God is finished**.*

In Revelation 16:1-2 we see the first bowl of wrath being poured out. It is poured upon those with the mark of the beast. We know this is during the Great Tribulation Period after the antichrist has been revealed. This first bowl occurs well before the Revelation 14 and 19 second advent passages that we just looked at (remember that Revelation is non-linear). The 7th bowl is when wrath is complete at the end of Armageddon.

In Revelation 16:10-16 we notice the 5th and 6th bowl judgments being poured out on the beast's kingdom and the gathering at Armageddon. As a side note, the 5th trumpet mentions a 5-month period in <u>Revelation 9:10</u>. This leads us to believe that the Day of the Lord and wrath being poured out is a long time (but less than 3.5 years).

We know bowl judgments follow the trumpets. If we use a likely option that the first bowl intensifies the first trumpet, we can connect bowls and trumpets to the Day of the Lord with the signs from the 6th seal and related passages such as <u>Joel 3:11-16</u>.

There are many reasons that the first bowl is unlikely to follow the 7th trumpet that we reviewed in Chapter 22. We can assume the first bowl follows the first trumpet, etc.

Since we also know saints are with Christ at the last battle in <u>Revelation 17:14</u>, we can assume that the rapture occurs towards the end of the wrath period, at the last trumpet, just before the last bowl is completed. Bowls follow trumpets slightly and intensify their calls. This leads us to the view that an end-wrath rapture best describes the timing of the rapture. A post-trib rapture also describes good general timing, but it is hard to nail down the relationship between the 3.5-year tribulation to the rapture.

## Timing and Duration of the Second Coming

A related study from Chapter 17 reveals how quickly Christ appears from the initial signs to when He finally comes at the second advent. We know the tribulation period is years long, but there are many passages that state Christ deals out punishment and saves the saints quickly. The duration always seems short since there are no references to drawn out battles. He speaks, and the wicked fall in a short breath. See 2 Thessalonians 2:8, Revelation 14:15-16, Revelation 17:14 and Revelation 19:19-21.

We have examined many reasons that timing and other complexities have challenged us to understand the book of Revelation and the second advent. By scratching the surface of textual comparison, we can be confident that the entire Bible is integrated to show common themes about the most important time in earth's history, the culmination of time. By going back to the Old Testament references, we know more about Christ's return, especially why He is coming.

Before we can learn details about when Christ comes back to earth, we should look to answer why He is coming back again. Could He not have destroyed the wicked and saved the saints at His first advent? He did to some extent to begin the process, but the promises were not fully realized. Hebrews 11:39-40 gives an answer based on the preceding verses of Hebrews 11.

We now arrive at potential discrepancies about Christ's first advent compared to His second. Some believe that death was destroyed once for all. 2 Timothy 1:10 states,

> *and which now has been manifested through the appearing of our Savior Christ Jesus, who **abolished death** and brought life and immortality to light through the gospel,*

Paul's statement to Timothy describes the first advent. Christ defeated death for Himself and brought it to light for us since He now holds the "keys" to death (Revelation 1:18).

Hebrews 9:26b *But as it is, he has appeared **once for all** at the end of the ages to put away sin by the sacrifice of himself.*

There are many other rabbit trails we can go down. We can revisit Hebrews 9:27-28. Verse 26 reports the first advent, while verse 28 states He "will appear a second time." In three verses we see the difference between the advents. He conquered sin once for all, but not death for us, yet.

We know the writer(s) of Hebrews stated we are living in the "last days" since the first advent (Hebrews 1:1-2). The only way we will know when we are at the end of the last days is by the signs discussed earlier.

Josephus did not write about the second advent in The Jewish War in Book 6, ch.5.3, regarding the destruction of the second_temple in Jerusalem. Full preterism does not consider the hundreds of passages that state destruction of all the wicked and salvation for the saints (like David, who is waiting for Christ to defeat all enemies so he can be resurrected (Acts 2:34-35)). Abraham is waiting as well (Hebrews 11:13-

16). Every tribe, nation and tongue is involved at the end (Revelation 1:7, Revelation 13:7, Revelation 14:6).

One issue we face is that there are passages with dual fulfillment. How do we know what was fulfilled already and what remains open? For example, Neo-Babylonians invaded the promised land then God judged them by sending the Persians to defeat them. However, some of these components also are stated in Revelation (such as Babylon is Fallen). Christ stated similarities to the destruction of the second temple (Luke 21:20-24) while including similar language for end times in a different sermon (Matthew 24:15-21).

Christ conquered death for Himself. We will not benefit from this until He returns, completely defeating death for all the saints in the process. We believe this concept of Christ defeating death as a similar dual fulfillment of prophecy. Death is defeated but not yet defeated.

1 Corinthians 15:16-26 is one that should lift our spirits.

*For if the dead are not raised, not even Christ has been raised. And if Christ has not been raised, your faith is futile and you are still in your sins. Then those also who have fallen asleep in Christ have perished. If in Christ we have hope in this life only, we are of all people most to be pitied.*

*But in fact Christ has been raised from the dead, the firstfruits of those who have fallen asleep. For as by a man came death, by a man has come also the resurrection of the dead. For as in Adam all die, so also* **in Christ shall all be made alive**. *But each in his own order: Christ the firstfruits, then* **at his coming** *those who belong to Christ. Then comes the end, when he delivers the kingdom to God the Father after destroying every rule and every authority and power. For he must reign until he has put all his enemies under his feet.* **The last enemy to be destroyed is death.**

# Chapter 25

## *What Is Judgment Day?*

There are two judgment days, each with different forms that should weigh on us as we contemplate the significance of what is bound to come. One is judgment upon the entire earth and the other is judgment of individual persons. The former begins on earth just before the second advent. This is toward the end of the Great Tribulation Period and during the Day of the Lord as the 6th seal is opened. The latter is after these initial events. There are good judgments for the righteous and bad judgments against the wicked.

We should remember that the resurrection and judgment events revolve around the second advent. Christ brings rewards and justice with Him at that time. Recompense is to repay that we see in Isaiah 35:4, 40:10, 59:17-20 and 62:11. These passages are simply repeated in Revelation 22:12 where Christ is bringing payment with him when He comes again (quickly / swiftly / without delay when He comes as in Isaiah 46:13, Hebrews 10:37 and Romans 9:27-28). Chapter 17 has more details about this concept.

Many second advent passages deal in judgments awarded and dealt out to a wide range of recipients. Saints, as true believers, can look forward to receiving eternal life and other rewards, while everlasting punishment awaits the wicked.

## Judgment for the Righteous

These passages speak to receiving rewards, crowns and other gifts that occur at His appearing and after – Isaiah 35:4, 40:10, 59:17-20, 62:11; Daniel 7:22; Matthew 16:27; Luke 14:14; 1 Corinthians 3:13-15, 4:5; 1 Thessalonian 2:19; 1 Timothy 6:19; 2 Timothy 4:8; Hebrews 9:27-28; 1 Peter 5:1-4; Revelation 2:10-11, 3:11-12, 22:12.

Matthew 19:27-29 is one of the most interesting summaries to examine regarding rewards. Surprisingly, this passage is not well known even though it sheds light not found elsewhere. Peter asked a question of Christ about His reward for following Him, then Christ made a direct comment about the regenerated world and his reward.

> Matthew 19:27-29 *"Then Peter said in reply, 'See, we have left everything and followed you. What then will we have?' Jesus said to them, 'Truly, I say to you, **in the new world**, when the Son of Man will sit on his glorious throne, you who have followed me will also sit on twelve thrones, judging the twelve tribes of Israel. And everyone who has left houses or brothers or sisters or father or mother or children or lands, for my name's sake, will receive a hundredfold and will inherit eternal life.'" v.28 thrones = Revelation 20:4.*

Here, we see the inheritance of eternal life and rewards being granted after Christ sits on the throne of glory at the time of judgment. This occurs at the new earth age after the cleansing and restoration. We need to know more about the timing and description of the world to come.

## The New Heavens and New Earth

The term "new" world means in the "regenerated" world or more commonly known as the "new earth" spoken of by Isaiah, Peter and John. Some may think this happens instantaneously, but it could take time to regenerate.

## Passages about the Regenerated Earth

Isaiah 65:17 = 66:22 = Acts 3:21 = Ephesians 1:9-10 = Revelation 21:1
=

Peter's further explanation – 2 Peter 3:13 *"But according to his promise we are waiting for new heavens and a **new earth** in which righteousness dwells."*

Does "new" have a quality of "like" new or "brand" new? Will the earth be a brand-new creation after Christ comes? No. "New" in this case is a renewal term of quality, not a time-based creation. Otherwise, there would not need to be any cleansing of the earth, as Christ could simply blow up the earth and start over. There would also be no need to bring the resting saints from Heaven to earth. The earth will need to be renewed like the former glory of Eden.

Matthew 19:28 carries us across the threshold in its reference to the "new world" in a clear context, so we know what Christ is referring to. Other passages use a generic term for "new" while Matthew leaves no room for doubt if it is a quality improvement or is time dependent. This crucial difference allows us to understand its greater significance when describing the coming transformation to the world.

## Passages about the Regenerated Earth

Most interestingly, the English translators have not standardized this "new" root word meaning "regeneration" – See the Greek root #3824. These are some English translations of the same Greek root word.

NIV – renewal

ESV – new

NASB – regeneration

KJV and NKJV – regeneration

NET – renewed

The only other usage of this same root word is found in Titus 3:5. Paul describes being born again by the Holy Spirit. This time, the ESV states the contextual term of "regeneration" but in Matthew 19:28 they utilized "new" in their translation.

Titus 3:5 *he saved us, not because of works done by us in righteousness, but according to his own mercy, by the washing of* **regeneration** *and renewal of the Holy Spirit,*

We see in many passages that the prophecies from the O.T. need to be fulfilled for complete restoration of earth.

> Acts 3:21... *whom heaven must receive **until the time for restoring all the things** about which God spoke by the mouth of his holy prophets long ago.*

A great example of redemption-restoration of the earth and our bodies is found in Romans 8:20-25. There is nothing brand new about the earth in Romans or this passage.

> 1 Corinthians 7:31 *and those who deal with the world as though they had no dealings with it. For **the present form of this world** is passing away.*

Apostolic expectations go back to the oaths made by God to Abraham about the promised land and his Seed inheriting and blessing the earth. It is an eternal promise that was never fulfilled, as we see in Acts 7:5 and Hebrews 11, with Abraham and all the O.T. saints still waiting for their promised land to be realized.

*Hebrews 11:10 For he (Abraham) was looking forward to the city that has foundations, whose designer and builder is God. 13 These all died in faith, not having received the things promised, but having seen them and greeted them from afar, and having acknowledged that they were strangers and exiles on the earth. 16 But as it is, they desire a better country, that is, a heavenly one. Therefore God is not ashamed to be called their God, for he has prepared for them a city. 39 And all these, though commended through their faith, did not receive what was promised, 40 since God had provided something better for us, that apart from us they should not be made perfect.*

This depiction of the kingdom on earth reveals the expectations of the apostles in Acts 1. The timeframe within the passage was after the resurrection of Christ and before His ascension into Heaven. The Jewish people had not forgotten about the eternal promises to Abraham that were passed on down.

*Acts 1:6-7... "Lord, will you at this time restore the kingdom to Israel?' He said to them, 'It is not for you to know times or seasons that the Father has fixed by his own authority.'"*

Christ could have said they will have the kingdom in their heart at Pentecost and their rewards will be paid out in Heaven when they died, but He didn't. If the disciples were satisfied about a spiritual reign of Christ in their hearts or a heavenly realm reign of Christ, they would have been jumping up and down after His resurrection. However, they knew a kingdom on earth was coming as clearly prophesied throughout the O.T. Their attitude in Acts 1:6 and Matthew 19:27 show they were still hoping for the kingdom not yet established.

## The Earth as an Inheritance

Matthew 5:5 states, *"the meek will inherit the earth."* This is a quote from Psalm 37:11 which is a repeat of the Abrahamic land promises.

Land = earth (i.e., "the meek will inherit the land").

Psalm 37:29 *"The righteous shall inherit the land and dwell upon it forever."*

135

Were David and Christ speaking literally about physical land or figuratively about heavenly bedrock? The interpretation method determines end time passages' meaning of Heaven coming to earth or us going to Heaven. Passages like Amos 9:15 are hard to ignore or discard. We should not state that land promise passages have been fulfilled on earth since the N.T. stated the promise is still open (Acts 7 and Hebrews 11).

In the literal land promise interpretation method (see Chapter 2 and Chapter 3) we find Christ coming back to earth, then there will be His heavenly kingdom physically established on earth. Heaven is where God dwells (whether He can be seen by eyes or whether He dwells in Spirit is another matter to discuss). A new earth ties the Bible together with God's plan for redemption, restoration, and renewal.

Romans 8:16-25, Ephesians 1:9-10, Hebrews 11:16 and 2 Peter 3:13 explain the Master's plan to merge the land promise with the heavenly kingdom. It is a uniting of the earthly + heavenly realms we see culminated in Revelation 21:1-4. Revelation also speaks to this merger, beginning with the 7th (last) Trumpet.

Revelation 10:7 *but that in the days of the trumpet call to be sounded by the seventh angel,* **the mystery of God would be fulfilled,** *just* **as he announced to his servants the prophets.**

11:15 *Then the seventh angel blew his trumpet, and there were loud voices in heaven, saying, '***The kingdom of the world has become the kingdom of our Lord*** *and of his Christ, and he shall reign forever and ever.'*

Christ has all authority in Heaven and on earth now (Matthew 28:18 and Ephesians 1:20-23), but He has not enacted all His authority on earth yet while He is reigning in Heaven. The earthly, physical reign will be announced at the 7th trumpet, then He comes to earth to cleanse it.

To understand why the earth needs to be cleansed, we need to go back and examine what the inheritance is all about. It includes earth and eternal life. Our eternal inheritance is living forever on earth. Earth was the original location where God intended to dwell with His creation.

Isaiah 45:18
*For thus says the LORD,*
*who created the heavens*
*(he is God!),*

*who formed the earth and made it*
*(he established it;*
*he did not create it empty,*
***he formed it to be inhabited!):***
*"I am the LORD, and there is no other."*

It is very clear that God created the earth for His purpose as stated in Isaiah 45:18, Colossians 1:16 and Hebrews 2:10 along with the fact that He did not just create the earth to give to Himself in the person of Christ but that He created the earth to share in it with us and live with us. This falls under the inheritance plan since we are co-heirs mentioned in Romans 8:16-17 with Galatians 3:29, stating we are Abraham's offspring.

> Galatians 3:29 *"And if you are Christ's, then you are Abraham's offspring, heirs according to promise."*
> This promise includes eternal life in the promised land.

## Cleansing of the Earth

Since it has been God's plan for us to inhabit the earth with Him, we now understand why He needs to judge the earth and cleanse it to establish His physical kingdom. The terms and phrases that describe this period give us vital insight into the circumstances and depictions surrounding the Day of the Lord. We need to go back to see how the cleansing concept developed to fully understand the message.

Cleansing is first mentioned in the Song of Moses. It is a prophecy of God's chosen people and the promised land. We notice this in the conclusion of this lengthy prophecy.

Deuteronomy 32:43

*"Rejoice with him, O heavens;*
*bow down to him, all gods,*
*for he avenges the blood of his children*
*and takes vengeance on his adversaries.*
*He repays those who hate him*
*and **cleanses his people's land**."*

We then see the theme continued throughout the prophets of the Old Testament such as Isaiah and Ezekiel. Isaiah combines attributes of the first and second advents in one passage.

Isaiah 4:2-6 *In that day the branch of the LORD shall be beautiful and glorious, and the fruit of the land shall be the pride and honor of the survivors of Israel. And he who is left in Zion and remains in Jerusalem will be called holy, everyone who has been recorded for life in Jerusalem, when the Lord shall have washed away the filth of the daughters of Zion and cleansed the bloodstains of Jerusalem from its midst by a spirit of judgment and by a spirit of burning. Then the LORD will create over the whole site of Mount Zion and over her assemblies a cloud by day, and smoke and the shining of a flaming fire by night; for over all the glory there will be a canopy. There will be a booth for shade by day from the heat, and for a refuge and a shelter from the storm and rain.*

Ezekiel chapters 36-39 describe the end of days and the cleansing of the earth at the time of the Day of the Lord and the resurrection of the dead. Here is a summary of what will occur after Armageddon when Christ comes to cleanse the land.

*Ezekiel 39:11-16 On that day I will give to Gog a place for burial in Israel, the Valley of the Travelers, east of the sea. It will block the travelers, for there Gog and all his multitude will be buried. It will be called the Valley of Hamon-gog. For seven months the house of Israel will be burying them, in order to cleanse the land. All the people of the land will bury them, and it will bring them renown on the day that I show my glory, declares the Lord GOD. They will set apart men to travel through the land regularly and bury those travelers remaining on the face of the land, so as to cleanse it. At the end of seven months they will make their search. And when these travel through the land and anyone sees a human bone, then he shall set up a sign by it, till the buriers have buried it in the Valley of Hamon-gog. (Hamonah is also the name of the city.) Thus shall they cleanse the land.*

Ezekiel then prophesies that Christ's feet will be placed on earth after the cleansing.

Ezekiel 43:7 *and he said to me, "Son of man, this is the place of my throne and **the place of the soles of my feet, where I will dwell** in the midst of the people of Israel forever. And the house of Israel shall no more defile my holy name, neither they, nor their kings, by their whoring and by the dead bodies of their kings at their high places,"*

Perhaps all these concepts are best summarized by Paul in Romans 8. Here he states the hope we have for the future, when all creation is restored at the revelation of Christ and His saints.

Romans 8:19-25 *For the creation waits with eager longing for the revealing of the sons of God. For the creation was subjected to futility, not willingly, but because of him who subjected it, in hope that the creation itself will be set free from its bondage to corruption and obtain the freedom of the glory of the children of God. For we know that the whole creation has been groaning together in the pains of childbirth until now. And not only the creation, but we ourselves, who have the firstfruits of the Spirit, groan inwardly as we wait eagerly for adoption as sons, the redemption of our bodies. For in this hope we were saved. Now hope that is seen is not hope. For who hopes for what he sees? But if we hope for what we do not see, we wait for it with patience.*

# Chapter 26

## Who Are the Sons of God in Genesis 6?

### Humanity's Relationship to the Spirit Realm of Fallen Angels

O ur journey to understanding how the beast fits within Revelation starts in Genesis 6, where we see how the fallen angels will affect the end times. We will revisit Genesis 3 later.

Genesis 6:1-4 *When man began to multiply on the face of the land and daughters were born to them, the* **sons of God** *saw that the daughters of man were attractive. And they took as their wives any they chose. Then the LORD said, "My Spirit shall not abide in man forever, for he is flesh: his days shall be 120 years." The Nephilim were on the earth in those days, and also afterward, when the sons of God came in to the daughters of man and they bore children to them. These were the mighty men who were of old, the men of renown.*

There are three dominant views regarding the famous Genesis 6 passage about the "Sons of God." Most Bible interpreters and commentators state that the godly children of Seth are the Sons of God marrying outside the faith, or that fallen angels mated with human women to produce giant offspring. We will expound our focus with a 3rd viewpoint presented by Meredith Kline, David Livingston, and others, while coordinating related biblical passages and mythology.

Our position begins with a brief statement made by Christ in Revelation 2:14.

> ...you have some there who hold the teaching of Balaam, who taught Balak to put a stumbling block before the sons of Israel, so that they might eat food sacrificed to idols and practice sexual immorality.

How does this passage in Revelation, written to an early Church, correlate with Genesis 6 or theories about fallen angels? There is a connection to idolatry from ancient times that we rarely consider today. We think of idolatry or pagan sacrificial systems as obsolete concepts. However, modern extensions are in practice today while escalating to the highest point in earth's history. We need to know how idolatry developed into current forms at national and individual levels.

We notice similar concepts about immorality and prostitution in Revelation Chapter 17 verse 2 – *[the prostitute] with whom the kings of the earth have committed sexual immorality...* Do we think that leaders of the earth would physically mate with the Mystery Babylon woman?

Often, biblical writers equate sexual immorality or prostitution in a figurative sense to mean unfaithfulness to God. There are many examples from Genesis 6 onward that associate humankind's relationship with false gods as a marriage. The outcome has always been infidelity against the true God.

God and His creations have a special bond that breaks with the worship of false gods. It is the equivalent of human adultery in the spirit realm. Trying to gain the benefits of a belief in God through ulterior means or through other sources is an exercise in futility that is bound to end up in failure.

<u>Hosea 5:4</u>

*Their deeds do not permit them*
*to return to their God.*
*For the spirit of whoredom is within them,*
*and they know not the LORD.*

Physically immoral acts are not as significant when compared to spiritual immorality, even if physical sex rituals of kings and queens, or priests and priestesses, are part of binding a nation to the demonic realm. The major problem is about people who turn their hearts against

God to receive gain from false gods. This can be through prayer, sacrifice, and other means.

We see a connection with false religious practices described throughout the Old Testament that shed light on Genesis 6. We can follow the breadcrumbs that are laid out for us in passages like Numbers 25:1-3.

> *While Israel lived in Shittim, the people began to whore with the daughters of Moab. These invited the people to the sacrifices of their gods, and the people ate and bowed down to their gods. So Israel yoked himself to Baal of Peor...*

Here we notice Israel being bound, or married, to a false god. This passage is explained in Psalm 106 within the context of offering sacrifices to demons.

> <u>Psalm 106:28</u> *Then they yoked themselves to the Baal of Peor, and ate sacrifices offered to **the dead;***
> <u>Verse 37</u> *They sacrificed their sons and their daughters to the **demons;***
> <u>Verse 39</u> *Thus they became unclean by their acts, and played the whore in their deeds.*

Baal worship is related to the passage we looked at in Revelation 2:14 and elsewhere in the Bible. Access to the evil realm is through demonic spirits of fallen angels. There have been many changes over time, so it is not Baal or names that we would consider as obvious today.

We should notice the relationship of the "dead" to "demons" in Psalm 106. The realm of the dead is called Sheol. This is a state of being more than a location. Sheol conveys a restricted nature of fallen angels after they rebelled against God. They are called shades, rephaim, and demons. All these terms are associated with the dead, yet the spirits of fallen angels have ability to influence the earth. We will see examples of how and why they affect people.

The ultimate rebellion is about other means to obtain eternal life than were originally intended. Fallen angels are defined by biblical terms of death, but their primary message is a lie about life. This goes back to Genesis 3:4 at the Garden of Eden and is the goal of all evil practices that try to bypass God's eternal life-giving plan. Certainly, humans have contacted demons for temporary gain, yet ancient cultures were greatly concerned about learning how to live forever. This has resulted in immortality myths passed down to modern times throughout the world.

We should know that the Bible reports extensively about divination, necromancy, and other practices seeking an alternative path around

God. It does not provide details about angelic beings that mated with humans to create hybrid offspring. Why should we focus on extracting details from unclear or sparse concepts when the majority of scripture speaks of union in a spiritual sense?

We know from Hesiod that ancient Greeks thought demons were good. Hesiod equated the spirits of titans bound to the realm of the dead with the demonic.

> *...they are called pure spirits dwelling on the earth, and are kindly, delivering from harm, and guardians of mortal men; for they roam everywhere over the earth, clothed in mist and keep watch on judgements and cruel deeds, givers of wealth...*
> – Hesiod. Works and Days, <u>Lines 109-139</u>

The Bible speaks in opposite terms about demons when compared to the Greeks. Demons are always presented in a negative light, since they distract humans from the true God towards selfish gain. We find the definition of demons as false gods first mentioned for us in Deuteronomy 32:17 –

> *They sacrificed to demons that were no gods, to gods they had never known, to new gods that had come recently, whom your fathers had never dreaded.*

Demons are synonymous with false gods in their primary meaning. The term "demon" was not used much in the Old Testament, but false gods were mentioned more frequently. Then there was a shift in terminology within the New Testament that commonly mentioned "demon" and "devil" in ways that have captured our common imagination. This evolution in how false gods are described is because of Greek conquest and Greek practices that remained dominant with the Romans during the first century. However, false god and demon core definitions remained synonymous in the New Testament.

Necromancy, use of mediums, and divination practices are attempts to contact the realm of the dead, whether higher-level beings or those believed to be ancestors. False gods, as demonic spirits, are considered dead according to the Bible, since they do not possess inherent immortality and are bound to death.

The realm of the dead was viewed as the afterlife in many ancient cultures, so it was not like we think of Heaven today. How did this view change? The Theological Dictionary of the New Testament has an answer to this eternal life changing question. Humans, and fallen angels, have skin in this game.

*"When the concept of the soul was further developed in the Greek world, a sharp distinction was made between the mortal body and the immortal soul which originates in the divine world. Only the latter journeys in the world to come. The idea of a journey of the soul now makes its appearance in Greek literature. According to the Orphic writings (6th – 5th century [BC]), which introduce the idea, the goal of souls is to return to their heavenly home after long travels. Hades now becomes the place of punishment, hell. Plato introduced into Greek philosophy the belief of the immortality of the soul and its many [re]incarnations up to the goal of final purification. According to the myth ... the soul goes to the place of judgment after leaving the body. There the judges order the righteous ... to ascend to Heaven ... The idea gradually changes from a descent of the soul to the underworld, to an ascent of the soul into Heaven."*

– Kittel, Gerhard. Theological Dictionary of the New Testament, Vol. VI, p. 568

Why would demons care where a human soul goes when he or she dies? Location is not a focus. The big lie is to get people believing they are as God. See Genesis 3:5 and notice the statements of pride in Isaiah 14:13-15 –

*... 'I will ascend to heaven;*

*… I will make myself like the Most High'.*
*But you are brought down to Sheol…*

Humans were not considered immortal in ancient times. The Bible states that God alone is immortal (1 Timothy 6:15-16) and that we are mortal at this time (1 Corinthians 15:51-53). There are no Bible passages stating our soul is immortal since we have conditional immortality. The condition is faith. We must believe in the One who grants immortality on the last day of the age (John 11:23-26).

Bodily resurrection from the dead was not a popular belief in ancient times. A spirit body resurrection to the heavens differs from the biblical model. Only those who had faith that God could raise them with a physical body believed in joining Him in the afterlife on earth. Job believed this as referenced in Job 19:25-27 and Abraham's faith about Heaven in the promised land is mentioned in Hebrews 11:8-16.

Generally, in the ancient world, gods and demi-gods were believed to have the ability to obtain immortality or could remain immortal, but not the average person. Gods died in many cases, and only worthy kings with their consorts could hope to pass through death to eternal life in the heavens. The average person hoped to have a peaceful existence in death. Certainly, the biblical message is better than the ancients, even though the concept of a resurrection seems foreign to most cultures such as shown in Acts 17:16-32. Is it harder to believe that we have an immortal soul bound to live in another realm after death, or a physical resurrection of an immortal body on earth?

All throughout the earth there were, and are remnants of, death cult practices. The Day of the Dead and All Souls Day show traces of them. Now there are many beliefs of inherent immortality for the average person. There has been a shift over time from everlasting death to eternal life. We can examine history to find that demons, through oracles and mediums, have promoted the spread of the immortal soul for all people to become the dominate view (see Barna Research – *Americans Describe Their Views About Life After Death*).

This brings us to the key points that are brought forward from the Old Testament into the New Testament, showing an unbroken chain of spiritual depravity.

## Humanity's Relationship with the Demonic Realm

**Rejection of Authority** – Both fallen angels and humans have rebelled against God. This creates a mutual affinity between rebellious people and the realm of evil. We see metaphors that associate rebellion to the worship of false gods in 1 Samuel 15:23.

*For rebellion is as the sin of divination, and presumption is as iniquity and idolatry.*

**Rituals** – Fallen angels' interaction with humanity is through their demonic spirits. Rituals are used by humans in attempts for earthly gain or gain towards the afterlife. The participants are fooled into believing they are performing good practices towards a true god. Even so, there is always the opportunity for them to repent and receive the gospel. We know that the Church in Thessalonica switched to the true God in 1 Thessalonians 1:9.

**Sexual Relations** – Sacred marriage rites bind humans with the fallen spirit realm. Sometimes there are physical acts that are part of the overall rites. However, most passages are concerned with spiritual infidelity against God using metaphors like adultery or prostitution. These can be considered in a figurative sense.

**Idolatry** – A physical idol can be seen but has no power without the unseen demon associated to it. Paul explains idolatry in 1 Corinthians 8 and in the first half of 1 Corinthians 10 with verse 20 stating –

*... I imply that what pagans sacrifice they offer to demons and not to God. I do not want you to be participants with demons.*

**Sacrifice** – Even child sacrifices are made in the name of false gods. Christ stated that hell shares the same name as the place Israel offered their children to Molech (ref. the Greek term of Gehenna that is reported in the N.T. is derived from Hebrew Hinnom).

Jeremiah 32:35 *They built the high places of Baal in the Valley of the Son of Hinnom, to offer up their sons and daughters to Molech, though I did not command them, nor did it enter into my mind, that they should do this abomination, to cause Judah to sin.*

**False Teaching** – Fallen angels taught heresies, such as promoting beliefs about humans being able to prolong their soul

153

within the realm of the dead or promoting heavenly ascension myths. These deceptions will increase during the last days in the Church. It is easy to point fingers at pagans, yet Paul warned Timothy in 1 Timothy 4:1 –

*Now the Spirit expressly says that in later times some will depart from the faith by devoting themselves to deceitful spirits and teachings of demons*

**Judgment** – upon the wicked fallen angels and human followers. God stated His judgement against the rebellion long ago, but the final sentence will not be fully executed until after the second advent. See Matthew Chapter 25 –

<u>Verse 31</u> *When the Son of Man comes in his glory, and all the angels with him, then he will sit on his glorious throne.*

<u>Verse 41</u> *Then he will say to those on his left, 'Depart from me, you cursed, into the eternal fire prepared for the devil and his angels.'*

These are the same concepts that are stated in Jude and 2 Peter, but the similarities don't stop there. Look at how the text reveals fallen angels in the realm of the dead.

Peter wrote in 2 Peter 2:4 *For if God did not spare angels when they sinned, but cast them into hell [lowest level of Hades known as the realm of the dead titans] and committed them to chains of gloomy darkness to be kept until the judgment*

Jude wrote in Verse 6 *And the angels who did not stay within their own position of authority, but left their proper dwelling, he has kept in eternal chains under gloomy darkness until the judgment of the great day*

Jude and 2 Peter chapters 2 and 3 are closely related, as shown in the table in Appendix 4 (or download at kjsoze.com/articles). By examining the corresponding Old Testament passages in the table, we realize that there are not any new concepts mentioned by Peter or Jude. They both summarize a common theme of rebellion that continually leads to greater selfishness. This will culminate with rebellion's ultimate expression at the end of this age.

## Differing Views About the Sons of God

To answer our original question, the Sons of God from Genesis 6 can be viewed as one of these options –

- Fallen angels that physically mated with women.

155

- The elect line of Seth that turned from God and became wicked.
- Men who claimed "Son of God" status through their relationship with the false gods of the fallen realm (demonic spirits). There was spiritual infidelity of angels with these wicked men who wanted more power.

Foremost, it should be noted that Christ is the only begotten Son of God. This means He was not created like any of the Sons of God options. Psalm 2:7 is repeated and expanded upon in Hebrews 1:5 –

> *For to which of the angels did God ever say, "You are my Son, today I have begotten you?" Or again, "I will be to him a father, and he shall be to me a son?"*

Angels are not inherently divine, even though they are sometimes called gods (Elohim). This brings us to our first option – fallen angels being called Sons of God in Genesis 6. An argument against this view is that Genesis 6:2 states that the Sons of God married the daughters of men. Christ stated that angels are not prone to marry in Matthew 22:30 *For in the resurrection they neither marry nor are given in marriage, but are like angels in heaven.* Perhaps these fallen angels are considered as gods who marry as one method to bypass Christ's determination. This defense does not explain the other issues with this theory.

What Christ stated in Matthew 22 is like early pagan writings about the demonic realm such as in Tablet 5 of *Utukku Lemnutu (UDUG HUL)* –

> 171 – *They are neither male nor female, ...*
> 173 – *they neither marry nor bear children.*

Certainly, many gods of ancient mythologies are reported to marry each other, but there are only later accounts such as in the 6th century BC of a god marrying a human (Dionysus and the daughter of King Midas).

Marriage is a key term to consider in Genesis 6 if we take it literally. There are a lot of examples of pagan gods having sexual relations with humans that report hybrid offspring like well-known demigods. Ancient gods from Mesopotamia or Egypt are not found to marry humans, even though human leaders often claimed a divine hereditary connection to a god. We should consider these claims as spiritual connections through demonic rituals, like Pharaoh's association with the false god of Horus, not that Pharaoh was a physical descendant of Horus, or Horus in the flesh.

There are more reasons why the option of angels physically mating with daughters of men is not likely. If the Sons of God in Genesis 6 were literally mating with humans, there should be more information presented elsewhere in Scripture. Perhaps the devil will increase this mythos in the coming days.

The bulk of information available in Scripture is related to demons as false gods and fallen spirits. There are hundreds of passages about these groups, with very few about the Sons of God within the context. There are no details of beings like Watchers that were created as higher entities above "regular" fallen angels, like the Book of Enoch presents. This book does not match the repeated theme of the Bible that speaks of demonic interaction through the spirit realm.

There are hierarchies of angels, yet no mention of little gods that are a class above angels. False gods and idols in Scripture are clearly associated with demons (spirits of fallen angels) that we examined in previous passages.

Here is a list of passages to consider where Christ, Job, Paul, and Peter had plenty of opportunities to explain any differences between the Sons of God and fallen angels or their spirits as demons.

> Luke 12:8 *And I tell you, everyone who acknowledges me before men, the Son of Man also will acknowledge before the angels of God,*

Job mentions Sons of God in verses like Job 1:6, but he does not mention angels. Conversely, he does not mention Sons of God in this passage below. There are no contextual passages in Job that differentiate the entities as separate beings.

> Job 4:18 *Even in his servants he puts no trust, and his angels he charges with error;*

Peter never mentions the Sons of God. He always refers to angels.

> 1 Peter 1:12 *It was revealed to them that they were serving not themselves but you, in the things that have now been announced to you through those who preached the good news to you by the Holy Spirit sent from heaven, things into which angels long to look.*

Hebrews 1 and 2 provide a lot of details about angels with no mention of the Sons of God. The writer(s) of Hebrews did not convey any different levels of angels. Instead, only a single type of entity named angels is mentioned, like most passages. Please read Hebrews 1.

This section concludes with Hebrews 2:5-10 where believers are made into sons of glory, like Paul's and Christ's teachings.

*For it was not to angels that God subjected the world to come, of which we are speaking. It has been testified somewhere, "What is man, that you are mindful of him, or the son of man, that you care for him?*

*You made him for a little while lower than the angels; you have crowned him with glory and honor,*

*putting everything in subjection under his feet." Now in putting everything in subjection to him, he left nothing outside his control. At present, we do not yet see everything in subjection to him. But we see him who for a little while was made lower than the angels, namely Jesus, crowned with glory and honor because of the suffering of death, so that by the grace of God he might taste death for everyone.*

*For it was fitting that he, for whom and by whom all things exist, in **bringing many sons to glory**, should make the founder of their salvation perfect through suffering.*

Based upon this extensive passage, we can understand more about angels and one reason why we were born. It is to be brought into glory as "complete" sons of God (i.e., a resurrected body). See 1 Corinthians 15:35-43.

Paul never reports on the Sons of God except as a term used to describe us with a spiritual connection to God, or physically describing us after the resurrection. He never compares Sons of God to angels.

Paul provides us with a summary in Romans 8, as he differentiates between a spiritual son of God compared to a physical son of God after the second advent (the timing of the bodily resurrection of the dead).

> <u>Romans 8:14-17</u> *For all who are led by the Spirit of God are sons of God. For you did not receive the spirit of slavery to fall back into fear, but you have received the Spirit of adoption as sons, by whom we cry, "Abba! Father!"*
>
> *The Spirit himself bears witness with our spirit that we are children of God, and if children, then heirs— heirs of God and fellow heirs with Christ, provided we suffer with him in order that we may also be glorified with him.*
>
> <u>Romans 8:23</u> *And not only the creation, but we ourselves, who have the firstfruits of the Spirit, groan inwardly as we wait eagerly for* ***adoption as sons, the redemption of our bodies.***

The end goal of humanity is the bodily resurrection of the dead. This is where we are told our bodies will be like angels (<u>Matthew 22:30</u>). Clear passages describe our resurrected body to be angelic, or Christ-like (Philippians 3:20–21). This is what we are to expect. We are told we will be glorified as children of God.

There are also more passages about our present state compared to the future concept of being a physical Son of God with our newly resurrected body at the second coming. Many passages support this hope.

> Philippians 3:20-21 *But our citizenship is in heaven, and from it we await a Savior, the Lord Jesus* **Christ, who will transform our lowly body to be like his glorious body,** *by the power that enables him even to subject all things to himself.*

One aspect related to glory is about "shining." This is an ancient concept that describes the Lord, the Angel of the Lord, and many other personages. We notice the saints' glorified, resurrected bodies as shining in Daniel 12:2-3 –

> *And many of those who sleep in the dust of the earth shall awake, some to everlasting life, and some to shame and everlasting contempt. And those who are wise shall* **shine** *like the brightness of the sky above; and those who turn many to righteousness, like the stars forever and ever.*

Christ states this shining concept will occur after the second coming mentioned in Matthew 13:43 – *Then the righteous will **shine** like the sun in the kingdom of their Father. He who has ears, let him hear.*

The devil lost his original light as he is now considered ruler over the darkness (Ephesians 6:11–12). He is associated with fallen angels (perhaps as a former cherubim or seraphim). He is also an accuser in several passages, but without any reference to his entity type in these legal settings.

Mark 3:22-23 *And the scribes who came down from Jerusalem were saying, "He is possessed by Beelzebul," and "by the prince of demons he casts out the demons." And he called them to him and said to them in parables, "How can Satan cast out Satan?"*

2 Corinthians 11:14 *And no wonder, for even Satan disguises himself as an angel of light.*

Revelation 12:7-9 *Now war arose in heaven, Michael and his angels fighting against the dragon. And the dragon and his angels fought back, but he was defeated, and there was no longer any place for them in heaven. And the great dragon was thrown down, that ancient serpent, who is called the devil and Satan, the deceiver of the whole world—he was thrown down to the earth, and his angels were thrown down with him.*

It is interesting to note that there could be some connection to the realm of the dead with giants. Rapha and Rephaim may be associated through the demonic practices of humans that produced giant offspring. We do not need to consider genetic manipulation without guidance from the biblical texts, yet we notice that demonic possession affects the physical traits of humans. Please see the Jewish Virtual Library for more information about the relationships between Rapha and Rephaim roots words.

What about the Divine Council from Psalm 82? Is it a type of high-ranking group of angels that are mentioned, or a separate class of beings like lower-level gods? We know there are hierarchies of angels with different purposes such as in legal matters or war (Daniel 10:11–14). They are called angels, archangels, or princes of angels.

Christ repeated Psalm 82 in John 10. There is no clarification about angels being synonymous with the Sons of God, or not.

> John 10:33-36 *The Jews answered him, "It is not for a good work that we are going to stone you but for blasphemy, because you, being a man, make yourself God." Jesus answered them, "Is it not written in your Law, 'I said, you are gods'? If he called them gods to whom the word of God came—and Scripture cannot be broken— do you say of him whom the Father consecrated and sent into the world, 'You are blaspheming,' because I said, 'I am the Son of God'?*

We know the ancients considered certain spirits as gods such as the medium of En-Dor (1 Samuel 28:13), or Hesiod reporting on the spirits of titan gods.

Another reason against the Sons of God as angels, or some higher-level entity, is the offspring produced mentioned in Genesis 6:4. They are the "mighty men" of renown. Mighty men are still men based upon the Hebrew root word usage. There is no mention of demigods or hybrid men like in mythology. The meaning is very clear when considering the context of Genesis chapters 6 and 10.

> Genesis 6:4 *The Nephilim were on the earth in those days, and also afterward, when the sons of God came in to the daughters of man and they bore* **children** *to them. These* **were the mighty men** *who were of old, the* **men** *of renown.*

We see this same "mighty" term used for Nimrod a few chapters later. There is more information to consider in Genesis 10:8, since this chapter is about human lineage after the flood. Nimrod is a man descended like normal men, even though he was the first mighty man (gibôr) after the flood. This would have been a perfect opportunity to call him a hybrid or some mixed bloodline.

> *Cush fathered Nimrod; he was the first on earth to be a mighty man.*

Nephilim are considered as big men. <u>Numbers 13:33</u> states that the Nephilim are giants. However, they are stated to be men, not hybrids. We know this from the root words and lineage of <u>Deuteronomy 9:1–2</u>.

In our final reason against the view of the Sons of God as fallen angels, in the context of Genesis 6, verses 3 and 5, judgment falls upon humanity, not angels. Separate punishment should have been mentioned to differentiate humanity from angels. This chapter is completely focused on mankind.

This brings us to the option of Seth's descendants as being the Sons of God in Genesis 6.

The only other passage written by Moses about the Sons of God is Deuteronomy 32:8-9. Here, they are specifically identified with the nations of the world, not God's chosen people. This is a perfect match to Genesis 6, which also references the world. Seth was part of the lineage to Noah and Christ, so his line was chosen out of the nations, not as part of the nations, just like we see with Jacob. There is a clear discrepancy between the identical Hebrew term if Sons of God are "the chosen" in one passage (Genesis 6) and not the other.

<u>Deuteronomy 32:8-9</u>
*When the Most High*
*gave to the nations their inheritance,*
*when he divided mankind,*

*he fixed the borders of the peoples*
*according to the number of **the sons of God.***
*But the LORD's portion is his people,*
*Jacob his allotted heritage.*

The opposite of Son of God is the son of the devil. We know this passage is not speaking of a physical descendent.

Acts 13:10 ... *"You son of the devil, you enemy of all righteousness, full of all deceit and villainy, will you not stop making crooked the straight paths of the Lord?"*

When we consider all related passages about being a son of good or evil, we notice it is a figurative term about a spiritual connection, not a physical lineage. There is only one literal case of Christ being the begotten Son of God and one future case of us sharing this title after the second coming.

By now we should have enough evidence to make the case that Genesis 6 confirms fallen angels had a spiritual relationship with the leaders of the earth prior to the flood. The leaders of that time are the Sons of God in this view. They sought control of territories through rituals with these demons. The offspring of the Sons of God were the "mighty men of renown" that brought forward traditions of demonic worship and ancestor worship. This is the same view that has support of many passages describing post-flood interaction between leaders and the demonic realm.

It was common in ancient times for kings to take as many wives as possible to expand their control and land regions. This unnatural power is an important aspect to consider from Genesis 6:1-4 with the rise of the city-state system. The practice of taking multiple wives is unnecessary, like it was long ago, yet the desire for control of territories and cultural beliefs remains. De Coulanges thoroughly describes this evolution in his book, The Ancient City.

Traditions of the expanded city-state continued after the flood as depicted by monuments and writings in stone tablets from post-diluvian history. It did not take long for the Tower of Babel event to re-institute these practices. Later, leaders like Naram-Sin of Akkad emerged as "God-King of the Universe." Many other leaders claimed a direct or indirect connection to the gods in order to control people.

Scripture records that pagan nations heavily influenced Israel in passages like 1 Kings 14:22-24, 2 Kings 17:7-12, Isaiah 57:3-9, Jeremiah 6:6-14, and Ezekiel 6:13. Many leaders in Israel's history acted as sons of gods, not as a son of the true God like David.

> Romans 8:14-16 *For all who are led by the Spirit of God are sons of God. For you did not receive the spirit of slavery to fall back into fear, but you have received the Spirit of adoption as sons, by whom we cry, "Abba! Father!" The Spirit himself bears witness with our spirit that we are children of God,*

There is also the future concept of us being a physical Son of God with our newly resurrected body. Many passages support this hope.

> Luke 20:36 *for they cannot die anymore, because they are equal to angels [non-fallen] and are sons of God, being sons of the resurrection.*

Luke 20:36 is the only verse found in Scripture that correlates being a son of God to angels. This is in reference to believers after a bodily resurrection (where immortality is granted). This passage could justify angels being Sons of God in Genesis 6. However, it is a rare instance and should not be used to contradict the many passages that speak of "sons of God" in a figurative sense, spiritual sense, or that have no direct correlation between different entities. The context of this passage is about humans and angels both having immortal bodies, not that angels are Sons of God as some distinct entity.

There are many types of sons, both spiritual and physical, but we shouldn't ever be confused by frivolous claims of kinship. Kings claimed to be sons of the gods. Angels are sons of God. Believers are spiritual sons of God and will be bodily resurrected to become sons of God. Christ is the only Son of God.

"Son of God" was a standard term used throughout the ancient world by leaders like Alexander the Great to establish authority over regions. His successors transferred his claim of authority to establish their own, even though his successors were not physical descendants. Divine rule continued in a magnitude of cases worldwide, like the Greek empire splitting into separate kingdoms or transferal of divine rites by Roman emperors.

Is divine rule or divine rite from the evil realm still in practice today? Who really cares if there is no connection to the average person? There are many levels of binding to evil spirits, so it is not usually a possession that needs an exorcism like Christ performed. Being bound to demons hides in the open under the guise of good. Even though we do not see a president or a prime minister sacrificing to gods today, we should be aware of other practices, even by average people. What gods do we worship today without knowing it? Are we aware of demonic influence surrounding us?

Some ancients thought their gods (demons) were good spirits that helped establish rule and order. Today, we have the same beliefs except we do not label these spirits as demons. Otherwise, we would not follow these beliefs. Remember who the father of lies is.

These lies are shown in the historical record to have developed over time from the performance of rituals to gain a better afterlife, to all souls being immortal, finally to the ultimate heresy where we are all gods. We will see the continued rise of this latter concept in the coming days. Can we look around us and see that people are becoming more self-centered?

The effects of being connected to the spiritual realm were well understood during the time of the New Testament. Although the titles and names have changed, we know evil forces are alive and active today. In modern times, we may use terms like nationalism, globalism, or ecumenicalism. You-know-who is behind it.

The apostle Paul wrote many times about these forces at work during the first century. We can bridge his terminologies to ours today.

## Passages by Paul About Spiritual Forces

See 1 Corinthians 15:24, 2 Corinthians 10:4, Ephesians 2:2, and

Ephesians 6:12 *For we do not wrestle against flesh and blood, but against the rulers, against the authorities, against the cosmic powers over this present darkness, against the spiritual forces of evil in the heavenly places.*

## As in the Days of Noah

It is relevant to understand Genesis 6 today. Even though there are not priest-kings today openly acting out ancient practices, there are the same principles at work. We need to look for the underlying "spiritual forces of evil." We should realize that Genesis 6:5 still holds true with the same core issue today.

> *The LORD saw that the wickedness of man was great in the earth, and that every intention of the thoughts of his heart was only evil continually.*

There is a lot of information available to study about this topic. One brief article that can be obtained easily is DIVINE KINGSHIP AND GENESIS 6:1-4 by MEREDITH G. KLINE.

Now we can better understand the background of Mystery Babylon and how false worship will be magnified at the end of this age.

*1 John 3:8-10 Whoever makes a practice of sinning is of the devil, for the devil has been sinning from the beginning. The reason the Son of God appeared was to destroy the works of the devil. No one born of God makes a practice of sinning, for God's seed abides in him; and he cannot keep on sinning, because he has been born of God. By this it is evident who are the children of God, and who are the children of the devil: whoever does not practice righteousness is not of God, nor is the one who does not love his brother.*

# Chapter 27

*What Is Mystery Babylon the Great?*

## The Rise and Continuation of the City-State System

While we've described some history about the demonic realm's influence over the nations on the earth, it's time to differentiate political and religious power within the human perspective. Mystery Babylon the Great is a symbol in the book of Revelation that depicts the depraved state of earthly leaders. Do we think empires, kingdoms, or city-states get weaker as time goes on, or is it the same system in operation with new clothes?

There have been many iterations of the evil realm that have interacted closely with human rulers. The relationship will amplify towards the end of this age. This is shown through symbology in the book of Revelation. Here, Babylon is described figuratively to mean all self-centered governments, businesses and religions on the globe.

Bible commentators have thought that Mystery Babylon is Rome, Jerusalem, or a restoration of ancient Babylon. Many interpretations have been derived from a vague passage by an angel describing the prostitute in Revelation 17 verse 18 –

*the woman that you saw is the great city that has dominion over the kings of the earth.*

The prostitute is also called Mystery Babylon, or Babylon the Great. The angel does not provide a complete answer in this short verse, so we need to know what the biblical definition of "city" is. Is there a literal city with powerful people working behind the scenes to control rulers over the earth, or is the city symbolic? We will focus our attention on the symbolic.

Throughout history, we notice that many kings and other leaders had unnatural desires to expand their control, wealth, and land regions. It seems that they were never satisfied. This hunger for more power is an important aspect to consider in Genesis 6:1-4 and Genesis 10:8-12. These passages describe the rise of the city-state system before and after the flood. The practices of taking multiple wives or building towers are not necessary like they were long ago, yet the desire for control of territories and people remains.

Scripture records that pagan nations heavily influenced Israel to subscribe to the city-state system in passages like 1 Kings 14:22-24, 2 Kings 17:7-12, and Isaiah 57:3-9. These examples show the worship of false gods, described as demons in Deuteronomy 32:17. We may think that the demonic realm only affected religious practices, but we know the political sphere was integrated with religion through priests and kings. There is a wide range of historical records with priest-kings in Sumer, Egypt, Greece, and Rome.

Looking forward, there are only two conclusive cities during the last days of this age and the beginning of the next age, according to Scripture. One is the city that God builds as everlasting, while the other is the city that humanity builds, only to be destroyed toward the end of our age. Obviously, Mystery Babylon is the symbolic city that man builds, since there are no good qualities of the woman who rides the beast in Revelation 17, or any righteous characteristics found in Revelation 18.

We know Christ went to "prepare a place" for us mentioned in John 14:3. We also know this is a dwelling place man will not build from Nathan's prophecy in 1 Chronicles 17 verses 9 and 10. There is no human effort achievable to build anything of lasting value when compared to what only God can build for us.

We will see this city called New Jerusalem in the future based upon the vision of Revelation 21 verses 2 through 4. It is designed and built by God, with the most wonderful depictions mentioned later in Revelation Chapter 21.

The intent has always been for God to dwell with man using His means, not for people to build their own type of system to please Him (Acts 17:24-25), or to honor themselves. The bad news is that humanity has continually asked for help through alternative means from the demonic, whether knowingly or unknowingly.

What we are concerned with in this study is the figurative city that man has constructed over thousands of years. This concept started with a literal city built by Cain (Genesis 4:17) and grew into a bigger concept after the flood.

> Genesis 11:5 – *And the LORD came down to see the* ***city*** *and the tower, which the children of* ***man had built***.

Many well-documented attempts in history display a theme of establishing self-interest for the elite through development of religio-political systems. Livy provides details in *The History of Rome,* Book 1. He uncovers how wealthy families got their power through myths and their association with the gods. Ancestral tradition (mos maiorum) then built the war machine.

Book 1 – *[7] Such traditions as belong to the time before the city was founded, or rather was presently to be founded, and are rather adorned with poetic legends than based upon trustworthy historical proofs, I purpose neither to affirm nor to refute. It is the privilege of antiquity to mingle divine things with human, and so to add dignity to the beginnings of cities; [8] and if any people ought to be allowed to consecrate their origins and refer them to a divine source, so great is the military glory of the Roman People that when they profess that their Father and* **the Father of their Founder was none other than Mars***, the nations of the earth may well submit to this also with as good a grace as they submit to Rome's dominion...*

The prophets Isaiah and Ezekiel tell us the foundational meaning of Mystery Babylon that Rome was involved in. We can trace their inspired words of Isaiah 47 and Ezekiel 27 to clear parallels of the "city of man" in Revelation 18. In these 3 chapters, we notice many attributes that encompass Mystery Babylon being built by humankind's efforts, but with the help of demons.

There are dual fulfillment prophecies in the Bible that we need to know about concerning past and future kingdoms. For example, Isaiah pointed to a near-term destruction of Babylon in Isaiah 47, but he also envisioned an ultimate destruction of Mystery Babylon. Revelation 18 echoes his vision that applies to the end of our age, when all human attempts are thwarted.

The bookends of Chapter 18 speak of demons in verse 2 and sorcery in verse 23. Humanity's efforts are throughout the rest of the chapter within this sphere of influence. These city-states, with their financial and military systems, could not be built without the help of the demonic realm.

Ezekiel also speaks to this dual fulfillment in Chapter 27 of his book. Tyre is the city-state of reference in this passage. It traces back through ancient Canaanite cultures to the Phoenicians of his period. The important point for end-time prophecy is that this vision is repeated in Revelation 18 with much of the same language.

Tyre is mentioned to be involved with wealth building, slave trade, and other prideful acts of the elite classes that are summarized in Ezekiel 27:33. These attempts by groups of power-hungry people have led to political and religious control over multitudes. Do we see this same type of system in place today? Yes, and this control system will only become more tyrannical in the coming days.

We find the source of the religious-political theme when we compare Isaiah and Ezekiel with Revelation Chapter 18. After the demon reference in 18:2 to set the table, we see leaders drink from the same cup. Please note that sexual immorality is spiritual, not a physical act in these cases. These elites of the earth share the spirit of demons by partaking of their depravity, and from these acts and demonic beliefs, their city-states and armies are positioned to grow stronger through the global networks of the beast system.

> Revelation 18:3 *For all nations have drunk the wine of the passion of her sexual immorality, and the kings of the earth have committed immorality with her, and the merchants of the earth have grown rich from the power of her luxurious living.*
>
> 18:7a *As she glorified herself and lived in luxury*
>
> 18:9a *And the kings of the earth, who committed sexual immorality and lived in luxury with her*

We can surmise that John's vision in Revelation draws from the same source as Ezekiel's and Isaiah's visions. It is the Holy Spirit. We can learn from all three chapters that the city-state system has been in operation for a long time and that it is called by different names. However, the details remain the same as shown in Appendix 5. Wealth building and luxurious living for the elite are common themes that are associated with the demonic realm.

The background of Mystery Babylon is also mentioned in Revelation 17. A prostitute is presented as the symbol for the city-state. This does not reflect literal adultery between her and the nations of the earth, since it is spiritual harlotry. It is likened to a wife selling herself when it is not needed because she has a husband. The Bible often uses prostitute terms for people bonding with demons (false gods – see Psalm 106:28-39). This is unnatural since the bond was meant for God and His bride (see Isaiah 49:14-18, Isaiah 62:1-5, Revelation 19:7-9, Revelation 21:2-9).

The table in Appendix 6 compares Revelation 17 verses related to the wicked-state with other referenced passages. Like Revelation 18, John's vision is shared by the Holy Spirit as He did with Jeremiah, Daniel, and others.

A common theme of Revelation chapters 17 and 18 is the mother city-state's association to the demonic realm bonding with the nations of the earth. This is a merger of an unholy church and state that has been occurring since the time before the flood. The religion used can vary. The common thread is that there have been leaders to control the masses and amass wealth.

Why would humans knowingly consult demons? Demons were often considered the good spirits of gods or ancestors in ancient times (see *Hesiod. Works and Days,* Lines 109-139). People believe the lie that has developed since Genesis 3's first lie.

Christianity has demonized demons in the West, so they now hide in the open hearts of people. There is no necessity for a king or president to join the occult and make a sacrifice on an altar to false gods. Alignment with the spirit realm can be through a person's heart that has selfish desires. This has always been the case, even though demons have gone "underground."

Humans and demons share the same selfish ambitions.

> Mark 7:21-23 – *For from within, out of the heart of man, come evil thoughts, sexual immorality, theft, murder, adultery... All these evil things come from within, and they defile a person.*
>
> John 8:44 *You are of your father the devil, and your will is to do your father's desires. He was a murderer from the beginning, and does not stand in the truth, because there is no truth in him. When he lies, he speaks out of his own character, for he is a liar and the father of lies.*
>
> James 3:14-16 *But if you have bitter jealousy and selfish ambition in your hearts, do not boast and be false to the truth. This is not the wisdom that comes down from above, but is earthly, unspiritual [opposite of good spirits], demonic. For where jealousy and selfish ambition exist, there will be disorder and every vile practice.*

There is direct or indirect contact with demons, deliberate or unknowing. However, in all cases, it boils down to selfish desires. Whether it be greed, lust, immoral ambition, or hunger for power, all leaders who have sought control over people for their own gain will be castigated in the end.

Today, we have global conglomerate corporations, an industrial-military complex, a pharmaceutical-medical complex, centralized global banking, and many corrupt governments around the world. It looks like the prostitute has been doing exactly what the Bible predicted. Nations that rely on these means of wealth generation will see an abrupt halt according to several passages in Revelation, including the 6th seal.

> Revelation 6:15 *Then the kings of the earth and the great ones and the generals and the rich and the powerful, and everyone, slave and free, hid themselves in the caves and among the rocks of the mountains,*
>
> 6:17 *for the great day of their [God's] wrath has come, and who can stand?*

We should notice that the 6th seal has similar language to Revelation 18. This is the end of the corrupt city-state and time for the wrath of God to come during the Day of the Lord period. Isaiah 2 also links these two chapters together with the same prophecies in verses 17 through 21.

> *And the haughtiness of man shall be humbled,*
> *and the lofty pride of men shall be brought low,*

*and the LORD alone will be exalted in that day.*
*And the idols shall utterly pass away.*
*And people shall enter the caves*
*of the rocks and the holes of the ground...*
*In that day mankind will cast away*
*their idols of silver and their idols of gold,*
*which they made for themselves to worship...*
*from before the terror of the LORD,*
*and from the splendor of his majesty,*
*when he rises to terrify the earth.*

The prostitute city-state system will end as predicted in Revelation 17:16 – *And the ten horns [kingdoms] that you saw, they and the beast will hate the prostitute [Mystery Babylon]. They will make her desolate and naked, and devour her flesh and burn her up with fire.*

Even though the beast of Revelation with its 10 kingdoms destroys the city-state system, it is because of God's judgment.

> Revelation 18:8b *and she [prostitute] will be burned up with fire; for mighty is the Lord God who has judged her.*

We then notice the Babylon city-state beneficiaries mourning the death of their gravy train (Revelation 18:16-19). The loss of control and wealth will be immense. Perhaps now we better understand why God's judgments will be so severe. The evilest people on the planet will be brought low by His just measures.

The timing of Armageddon and other Day of the Lord events mentioned in Revelation have not yet occurred when Mystery Babylon is destroyed. In the end, it is the beast vs. God. We know who wins.

While the truth about when Armageddon will occur is joined to the second coming, we can't overlook the significance of the other relationship between the beast and the harlot city-state prior to this age event conflict. The relationship is reflected by the beast and its symbolic heads.

The prostitute of Revelation is not a city-state like Rome because of the 7 heads on the beast she is identified with. She was active at all stages of the "high places" in history. The timing for her and one of the beast heads is visible during the 1st century.

## The Relationship of the Beast to Mystery Babylon

- The beast, in its entirety, was not active when John wrote the book of Revelation. Chapter 17 verse 8 – *The beast that you saw was, and is not, and is about [going] to rise from the bottomless pit and go to destruction.*

- Only one head of the beast was active when John wrote Revelation. Chapter 17 verses 9 and 10 -... *the seven heads are seven mountains on which the woman is seated; they are also seven kings, five of whom have fallen, one is, the other has not yet come...*

This shows us that the 6th head of the beast is the demonic link to the city-state of Rome, but the beast in its entirety does not have complete authority on earth until the end of the age (Revelation 13:4).

We also see in Revelation 17:9-10 that Mystery Babylon the Great has been active for a long time, since she has been part of the relationship with the devil during each of the heads of the beast. Rome was only one period that she was connected to. Her being seated on the beast with the 7 heads depicts her continued affiliation to the demonic realm throughout history.

The last head of the beast is the completion of spiritual interaction to the city-state system of man. The human race will lose all "control" when the 10 kingdoms of the earth hand their authority over to the beast. Then the devil will not need a "middle-man." He will have direct access to people towards the end of this age we live in. However, we must remember that God allows this to happen for His plans to be fulfilled.

Revelation 17:17 *for God has put it into their hearts [10 kingdoms] to carry out his purpose by being of one mind and handing over their royal power to the beast, until the words of God are fulfilled.*

# Chapter 28

*What Is the Beast of Revelation?*

## The Symbol of the Beast is Explained in Revelation 17

Who, or what, is the beast of Revelation? The danger of getting lost in the metaphor feels tangible when contemplating the Bible's foremost threats to humanity. But we cannot know the Mark of the Beast or any other details until we trace the history of kingdoms, both spiritual and earthly. The end-time beast can be considered as a spiritual kingdom, or the driving force behind religious-political systems on earth.

This evil spirit beast we are looking at is not the antichrist mentioned in Daniel, 2 Thessalonians, or Revelation that describes a person. That topic will be discussed further in the *"Who is the Antichrist?"* chapter.

We first need to look at Daniel chapters 2 and 7 so we can see the difference between earthly and spiritual kingdoms. After studying the original context, we can understand the beast of Revelation.

We begin with Daniel 2:31-45 – this section primarily comprises earthly kingdoms. It ends with the heavenly kingdom being firmly established on earth. The passage describes the famous statue vision of Nebuchadnezzar that is interpreted through Daniel.

There are five successive earthly kingdoms in the vision. We are focused on the fourth and fifth because they are important to know later for our comparison of Daniel to Revelation. The first three are historical and have no direct impact within end times. The fourth kingdom is ancient Rome, which has more of an impact.

The fifth kingdom's interpretation explains the feet and toes of the statue. The toes do not mean ancient Rome is revived in the end times, even though there is still iron present in the feet of the statue vision. The toes are a distinct kingdom from Rome's legs of iron, but there is an interesting association that we will examine later in Daniel 2:40-41 and in Revelation 17.

> The relationship to end times is referenced in verse 34 of Daniel Chapter 2 – *As you looked, a stone was cut out by no human hand, and it struck the image on its feet*

Christ's kingdom is the "stone." This Stone strikes the feet at the second coming. The beast with the evil kingdoms of the earth and the antichrist are destroyed at Christ's next advent.

We know from Revelation 17:12 that ten kingdoms, described as horns, are futuristic from the time when John penned Revelation. After considering all related passages, we can infer that the 10 horns of Daniel 7, Revelation 13, and Revelation 17, along with the 10 toes of Daniel 2, are the same group of ten symbolic kingdoms contemporaneous to each other within the end times.

Next, we see the stone turning into a mountain that becomes the eternal kingdom physically established on earth. However, this mountain is not heavenly Mount Zion that exists today, such as referenced in Hebrews 12:22.

> In verse 35 of Daniel 2, we notice – *the stone that struck the image became a great mountain and filled the whole earth.*

There are other passages that describe Christ's heavenly kingdom as it stands today. We should understand the differences between Christ's present reign compared to His future reign on earth. The disciples knew that the kingdom on earth was yet to come (Acts 1:6-11) even though He began His kingdom during the first advent.

Filling the whole earth with Christ's physical kingdom is part of the inheritance theme described throughout Scripture. It is the promised land fulfilled at last. We do not need to speculate if it was fulfilled figuratively in the Old Testament or the first century. This topic is thoroughly described in Hebrews 11:8-16. There are also brief references like Psalm 37:29 repeated in Matthew 5:5. Christ literally grants the completed land promise of heaven on earth just after the second advent, after the beast is destroyed.

Next, we see Daniel explains the differences between the fourth and fifth kingdoms as he interprets the vision of the statue. Rome is portrayed as the iron empire since it did exactly what Daniel described as the fourth kingdom.

> Daniel 2, verses 40 and 41 – *And there shall be a fourth kingdom, strong as iron, because iron breaks to pieces and shatters all things. And like iron that crushes, it shall break and crush all these. And as you saw the feet and toes, partly of potter's clay and partly of iron, it shall be a divided kingdom...*

Based upon verse 44, the timing of the second coming can be firmly established to occur during the fifth kingdom of ten toes. This is when the stone crushes the statue, and the mountain of God fills the whole earth.

> Verse 44 ***And in the days of those kings*** *[10 toes] the God of heaven will set up a kingdom that shall never be destroyed, nor shall the kingdom be left to another people. It shall break in pieces all these kingdoms and bring them to an end, and it shall stand forever.*

Daniel 2:44 describes the identical kingdom with the same timing as Daniel 7:22 and Daniel 7:27. We need to keep this important marker in mind if we are to understand Revelation, since these prophecies repeat. Daniel used different metaphors, but they have the same meaning of New Jerusalem coming from Heaven to be established on the newly restored earth (Revelation chapters 19 through 22). "New" is literally rendered from the original Greek text as the "regenerated" earth that Christ prophesied in Matthew 19:28. Eden Part 2 is a reoccurring theme we need to keep in mind.

Daniel 7 also deals with the fourth and fifth earthly kingdoms mentioned in Daniel 2. Here we visualize ancient Rome morphing into something that Chapter 2 explained little about. The 10 toes are described as 10 horns in verse 7 of Daniel Chapter 7 –

> *... behold, a fourth beast, It had great iron teeth; it devoured and broke in pieces and stamped what was left with its feet. It was different from all the beasts that were before it, and it had ten horns.*

Iron is mentioned in the fourth beast, which is associated with Rome. We notice its transition from the old Roman empire splitting into many power centers (horns) of the fifth kingdom. This occurs over hundreds of years until the completeness of ten comes at the end of the age. Ten symbolizes the entire earth, even though this group is described as divided nations. In the end, they agree to hand all their authority over to the devil's empire of the beast (see <u>Revelation 17:17</u>). A separate discussion will examine Rome's collapse and a resulting global dust cloud effect that morphs into unity at the end of days.

There is no need to figure out which ten countries or what ten leaders comprise the last kingdom on earth. The Bible does not hint of a necessity for an earthly power like a European Union or United Nations to take over the world. We should hold to the fact that Daniel stated the ten are "divided" nations. They do not bond well, but they will be like-minded. Their solidarity will be to relinquish their power to the antichrist.

The fourth and fifth kingdoms are different, as we notice in verses 23 and 24 of Daniel 7 –

> ... *As for the fourth beast, there shall be a fourth kingdom on earth...*
>
> *As for the ten horns, out of **this kingdom** ten kings shall arise...*

"This kingdom" refers to the ten horns of the fifth kingdom, not the fourth beast of the ancient Roman empire that was described previously as having iron. This passage shows us that Rome will not be revived during the end times, even though there is some association.

Next, please take careful notice of another important concept mentioned in verse 11 of Daniel 7 – ... *And as I looked, the beast was killed, and its body destroyed and given over to be burned with fire...*

Daniel 7:11 parallels Revelation 19:19-20 with identical terms of the beast, including the ten horns being destroyed by fire. These related passages verify consistency to the period of the second advent when the stone crushes the ten toes.

It might seem anti-climactic to say the beast is destroyed in the form of the antichrist at the end of this age, but we can't confuse the validity of the Bible with the twists and turns found in Hollywood movies. The antichrist is a person who dies, while the beast spirit inside him will reap spiritual death of the devil's influence over the earth. Only Christ will reign forever after with His saints.

It is interesting to note that the previously mentioned beast kingdoms of Daniel 7:4-6 will exist during the heavenly kingdom of Christ that He will establish on earth. Even though national leadership will be destroyed, peoples from all nations remain on earth during the judgment period of Christ's reign on earth. These are called survivor nations (Isaiah 45:18-23).

> Verse 12 of Daniel 7 reports this -... *As for the rest of the beasts, their dominion was taken away, but their lives were prolonged for a season and a time.*

There are Old Testament passages about nations being active and bringing tribute to New Jerusalem in the messianic kingdom of the "new" heavens and earth. See Isaiah 60 and Isaiah 66:18-23. These prophecies are the same as John's vision in Revelation 21:1-3 and Revelation 21:22-27.

Psalm 2:8, Daniel 7:14 and Colossians 1:12-16 provide us with background that Christ receives the entire earth, then shares with us the inheritance of the promise that began with Abraham.

We know Christ's physical kingdom will be located on earth based upon Matthew 19:27-29, 2 Peter 3:13 and in verse 27 of Daniel 7 –

> *And the kingdom and the dominion and the greatness of the kingdoms **under the whole heaven** shall be given to the people of the saints...*

Christ has authority to grant the promised land referenced in Daniel 7:27 based on the earlier verse of Daniel 7:14 –

> *And to him was given dominion*
> *and glory and a kingdom,*
> *that all peoples, nations, and languages*
> *should serve him;*
> *his dominion is an everlasting dominion,*

*which shall not pass away,*
*and his kingdom one*
*that shall not be destroyed.*

In the next section, we move from Daniel to the Book of Revelation.

## The Beast of Revelation 13 and Revelation 17

We start by examining the beast of all beasts, the dragon of Revelation. We will see his relationship to the final beast kingdom that we examined in Daniel Chapters 2 and 7.

| Summary of the Unholy Trinity |
| --- |
| The dragon is a fallen angelic being and leader of the rebellion |
| The beast is his spiritual influence over the earth |
| The antichrist is possessed by the devil through the beast |

Early in Revelation Chapter 12, we notice activity of the devil at the time of Christ's first advent with a description of him as the dragon. Verse 3 states –

*And another sign appeared in heaven: behold, a great red dragon, with seven heads and ten horns, and on his heads seven diadems*

To remove any doubt who the dragon is, John's vision describes the executioner of evil in Revelation 12 verse 9.

*And the great dragon was thrown down, that ancient serpent, who is called the devil and Satan, the deceiver of the whole world—he was thrown down to the earth*

There is something different about this great beast from the final beast mentioned in Daniel. The dragon has seven heads, where no beast has seven heads in Daniel. This may mean the devil is not mentioned in these chapters of Daniel. However, Revelation extends Daniel's original vision by providing us with more information. Seven is a complete number in Scripture, so the devil's heads convey his complete reign over evil, from Eden to the end of the age.

Next, we notice a seven-headed beast in Revelation 13. The beast of Revelation was fully active earlier in earth's history and will return in the last days. This differs from Daniel. Each beast of Daniel represents an individual kingdom period throughout the stages of history. The seven-headed beast reveals Daniel's beasts as a composite and the culmination of Daniel's fifth kingdom of ten horns.

The major difference between the fifth kingdom of Daniel and the beast of Revelation is that there are no heads in Daniel's. However, the similarities that are mentioned provide evidence of the transition of all previous beasts to the end-time system of the final beast.

## Similarities of Daniel's and Revelation's Beasts

A bridge between the 5th kingdom of Daniel and the beast of Revelation 13 is the 10 horns. This is a key to understand the rise of the beast.

The antichrist is associated with the last form of the beast in Daniel and Revelation. Both chapters speak of a great "mouth" that blasphemes God. The mouth emerges out of the last beast (Daniel 7:8, 7:11, 7:25, and Revelation 13:5-6).

Under the power of this beast, the antichrist is allowed to temporarily conquer the saints. This is until Christ comes after the tribulation period. See Daniel 7:21-22, Daniel 7:25-26, and Revelation 13:7.

Daniel and Revelation both show that the end time beast is destroyed with fire (at the second advent)

The fifth kingdom of Daniel is not a normal kingdom since it is divided and stems from the fourth beast. The first four beasts were typical empires. The collapse of Rome did not produce a unified empire, although Charlemagne and others tried. However, there is a transition from the fourth beast to the addition of ten horns, then to the final beast empire form.

What is the relationship of the dragon to the beast? The heads of the dragon represent complete reign of the devil himself over earth's history, while each head of the beast represents the devil's spiritual interaction during the corresponding kingdom's period. This interaction is through the Prostitute of Revelation 17:3 who represents mankind's religious-political connection to the devil through these respective kingdoms.

The final beast is also a composite of all beasts mentioned in Daniel 7 (Revelation 13:2). It is a picture of the ultimate beast, a summation of all kingdoms under the devil's authority throughout time since the fall.

The beast is depicted as the dragon's last kingdom that rules until the times of the Gentiles are fulfilled, when Christ comes to deliver the promised land (Luke 21:24-27). The final beast is not complete until the Great Tribulation Period begins, when it rises from the pit (Revelation 11:7, Revelation 17:8).

The beast rises out of the abyss, with "pit" sharing the same meaning. It also rises out of the symbolic universal sea. Daniel 7 and Revelation 13 speak of the beast coming out of this sea, while Revelation 17 conveys the beast of Revelation 13 rising out of the pit. The places where this beast rises from are different terms, yet it is still the same beast, since they are symbolic locations. The pit means death, while the sea means the entire nations of the earth. Both meanings are correct when we dig deeper into the original texts.

> Revelation 13:1 *And I saw a beast rising out of the sea, with ten horns and seven heads, with ten diadems on its horns and blasphemous names on its heads.*

After the devil is removed from access in the heavenly realm (Revelation 12:7-12), he receives authority to combine his spiritual beast kingdom with the divided kingdoms of the earth. The beast rises from the sea of these divided nations, but they will ultimately unify towards a purpose. They will have "one mind" with the beast (Revelation 17:13). This is the fifth beast of Daniel that gives up all its earthly power to the devil's final beast kingdom.

There were changes in the devil's authority from Eden, to Babel, to Rome, and onward. He started with the original authority he was given in Eden. This was diminished after the fall with his loss of direct access to the entire earth. He was then allowed indirect spiritual access. He will be granted full access again in the future. This will occur when he possesses the body of a human as the antichrist. Please see Appendix 7 for a table showing his authority throughout history.

The devil is presently allowed indirect authority on earth until Daniel 12:1, 2 Thessalonians 2:6-7 and Revelation 12:7-9 occur. These three passages are the same period when the devil's direct access to earth is reinstated. It is at the time when the beast rises from death. We know the entire beast was not active during the time of John, since the angel told him the beast "is not" (Revelation 17:8). Only heads of the beast have been active since the fall. This means that the devil has only been partially active on earth since the Garden. What will happen when he is fully commissioned to be physically present on earth? It will be worse than any previous events of history.

The devil will be granted authority on earth but only for a "short time" as mentioned in Revelation 12:12, with his followers receiving the same time constraint in Revelation 17:12. This authority is granted by God to complete all prophecies (Revelation 17:17). Ultimately, God allows this to fulfill his predetermined will of salvation.

Revelation 13:4 *they [people] worshiped the dragon,*
*for he had given his authority to the beast,*

All people on earth will see the devil's spiritual reign of the beast through the physical reign of the antichrist. This is after the 10 kingdoms give up control of the entire earth (Revelation 17:13). The Great Tribulation Period begins when this occurs. It is not limited to Israel or other local phenomena.

> Revelation 13:7 ... *authority was given it [the final beast] over every tribe and people and language and nation.*

## Does the Devil Have Power Over the Earth?

In Revelation Chapter 17, an angel explains more about the final beast to John. The vision starts with an image of a woman riding on it in verse 3 – *I saw a woman sitting on a scarlet beast that was full of blasphemous names, and it had seven heads and ten horns.* We should notice that the scarlet color of the beast is the same as the dragon. The other details of the seven heads and ten horns are also the same as Revelation chapters 12 and 13.

Next, we find confirmation that the beast was previously active on earth but not at the time of John.

> Revelation 17:8 *The beast that you saw was, and **is not**, and is about [going] to rise from the bottomless pit and go to destruction.*

Contrary to popular belief, the devil was not "living" on earth at the time of John. The only time that the devil seemed to have a physical body on earth was at the Garden of Eden. There is an interesting passage in the Gospels where the devil meets Christ, but it looks as if it was in spirit. Also, he entered Judas as a spirit (Luke 22:3), so these passages do not seem to point to a literal body. God considers fallen angels as being "dead." They do not have living bodies.

> Luke 4:5-6 *And the devil took him up and showed him all the kingdoms of the world in a moment of time, and said to him, "To you I will give all this authority and their glory, for it has been delivered to me, and I give it to whom I will."*

Interestingly, as related to our study, the "kingdoms of the world" concept mentioned in Luke 4 relates to the 7 heads of the dragon in Revelation. This Gospel passage confirms his granted authority. Even though the devil does not have a physical body here now, he rules the earth by the spiritual realm. Paul reports his evil spirit realm as cosmic, not earthly (Ephesians 6:12).

There are many examples throughout Scripture about individual kingdoms within a territory like Egypt or Assyria, but not any global empires until the future Great Tribulation Period. There is one unique empire we need to learn about regarding the individual head that was active during John's day. It is the only one that can explain the transition from Daniel's fourth beast to his vision of the fifth kingdom with ten horns.

The beast's heads are depicted as mountains. Mountains are "high places" mentioned in the Old Testament where humanity and the spiritual realm meet. Ancient Sumerian words like Ki and Kur often related Mountains to the underworld with gods and demons (see Sacred-Texts.com article about Ki and Kur).

The seven heads of the beast are not only spiritual meetings between humans and the devil, but are also seven kings or kingdoms that channel government towards evil. The heads are each based upon false religious and political systems during a kingdom period such as Babylon or Greece.

> <u>Revelation 17:9-10</u> *the seven heads are seven mountains on which the woman is seated; they are also seven kings, five of whom have fallen, **one is**, the other has not yet come, and when he does come he must remain only a little while.*

The sixth head in the succession is Rome, mentioned as the one that "is." This leaves one final earthly kingdom yet to come after John wrote Revelation. The 7th head is the evolution of Rome to the divided nations that are spread over the earth. They will come together with one mind of the antichrist after the beast rises out of the sea, as the devil is removed from the heavenly realm.

The passages that John wrote in Revelation relating to the coming kingdom of God are particularly prescient when we recall Rome was in power at the time and was known to be a pagan kingdom that openly worshipped false gods for earthly gain. Rome's beliefs trace back to the most ancient mystery religion, worship with the devil. While that's the topic for another book entirely, suffice it to say here that the original deception from Eden has carried on to this day through the spread of the Roman cult.

The final beast is part of a long chain of the devil's deception over major empires. This is because the beast is the spirit of the devil himself. The devil has interacted on earth directly through the serpent, then indirectly through spiritual influence over kingdoms. Only one head operated during any period, and the beast of Revelation is no exception. All heads relate to the beast during their time of power; however, we learn of an eighth head that connects them as part of the devil's spirit. He has been influential since Eden.

> Revelation 17:11 *As for the beast that was and is not, it is an eighth but it belongs to the seven, and it goes to destruction.*

This eighth head shows a transition from earthly based kingdoms to a pure evil kingdom led by the devil himself through the person of the antichrist. The 7th head is the last earthly empire of the ten horns before this final phase occurs.

The beast has always existed since the fall, whether in direct communication with humanity through a physical body or through the realm of the dead (demonic influence).

The ten toes, ten kings, and ten horns references are the global leaders that combine as one mind with the antichrist to complete the transition to the final beast. Remember that the fifth kingdom began as a mix of iron and clay (Daniel 2:41). They will crumble soon after they try to merge (Daniel 2:43). Humanity will not bond to the devil for long.

> Revelation 17:12-13 *And the ten horns that you saw are ten kings who have not yet received royal power, but they are to receive authority as kings for one hour, together with the beast. These are of one mind, and they hand over their power and authority to the beast.*

The end comes when all prophecies of this age are fulfilled during the second advent. Revelation 17:14 – *They will make war on the Lamb, and the Lamb will conquer them, for he is Lord of lords and King of kings, and those with him are called and chosen and faithful.* This prophecy was first described in Daniel 2:44 showing the 10 kingdoms being active at the second coming.

We see God's plan has been in place for a long time. <u>Revelation 17:17</u> – **God has put it into their** *[the 10 kings]* **hearts** *to carry out his purpose by being of one mind and handing over their royal power to the beast,* **until the words of God are fulfilled**

The only way Revelation can be understood is through context of the entire Bible with guidance from other passages such as from Isaiah, Daniel and Luke. We can strip away at the symbolism to find the literal meaning when we combine and compare all references.

The devil's kingdom is destroyed at the second advent – <u>Daniel 7:11</u> and <u>Revelation 19:19-20</u>. This ultimately means there will never be any type of reign of the devil when Christ comes to set up His permanent kingdom on earth (reference <u>Daniel 2:35</u>, <u>2:44</u> and <u>Daniel 7:27</u>). Only Christ will reign from that point, while he also grants authority for His saints to reign with him.

<u>Revelation 5:10</u> *and you have made them a kingdom and priests to our God, and they shall reign on the earth.*

# Chapter 29

*Who Is the Antichrist?*

## Identifying Daniel's Little Horn in Revelation

Many have tried to identify the antichrist with famous villains like Nero or Hitler. These attempts have failed. Perhaps it is because we have missed the obvious in the biblical text by looking for hidden details about some secret code or clue that does not exist. Let's try another perspective.

We begin our discussion of the antichrist with this person coming out of the beast, which we learned about in the previous chapter. It is important to remember that the beast is the satanic kingdom at the end of our age. He established a spiritual kingdom long ago that will resurrect into its final form as the person of the antichrist, a man who will expand the devil's reign of evil in the last days.

> Revelation 3:10 *Because you have kept my word about patient endurance, I will keep you from the hour of trial that is coming on the whole world, to try those who dwell on the earth.*

The greatest test ever will be the Great Tribulation Period that affects the entire earth (Daniel 12:1 and Matthew 24:21-22). People will align with the true God, or with the devil. The antichrist is the designated leader during this test period who arises out of the global system operated behind the scenes by the devil himself.

Before getting into the details, we should notice that God not only allows these events to occur but wills them to happen according to His plan. Romans 9:14-24 provides the background about God's predetermination that we need to understand regarding the book of Revelation.

> We see this concept about God's will for government in Revelation 17:17 – *for God has put it into their [world leaders] hearts to carry out his purpose by being of one mind and handing over their royal power to the beast, until the words of God are fulfilled.* Also, see 2 Thessalonians 2:11-12.

Why would God allow so much power to the devil acting through the antichrist? Quite simply, it is His plan to test the earth, so He uses everything to serve His purpose.

> Proverbs 16:4 *The LORD has made everything for its purpose, even the wicked for the day of trouble.*

Limited authority granted to the devil points back to Eden and the original rebellion against God. Afterward, we notice in Luke 4:5-6 that the devil had been granted temporary rights to the entire earth. 1 John 5:18-19 states the deep reach of his impact over the lives of all unsaved people.

> *We know that everyone who has been born of God does not keep on sinning, but he who was born of God protects him, and the evil one does not touch him. We know that we are from God, **and the whole world lies in the power of the evil one**.*

It is important to know the difference between the evil kingdom of the world and the Kingdom of Heaven. John explains the teachings of Christ about the devil and the world in many other passages, including these –

*John 17:14-15 I have given them your word, and the world has hated them because they are not of the world, just as I am not of the world. I do not ask that you take them out of the world, but that you keep them from the evil one.*

*1 John 2:15-16 Do not love the world or the things in the world. If anyone loves the world, the love of the Father is not in him. For all that is in the world—the desires of the flesh and the desires of the eyes and pride of life—is not from the Father but is from the world.*

We can't ever let it slip our minds that Christ created the world for His purpose and ultimately holds the reins over the world. We realize it is His intent to regenerate it through the cleansing process described throughout the book of Revelation. This is to fulfill the promised land prophecies that include bonus upgrades after the earth is transformed (Hebrews 11:8-16).

The devil and his minions will dispense God's judgment upon false religious-political systems of mankind. Revelation 19:2 states that this judgment is credited to God alone, while Revelation 17:16-17 reports how His sentence will be carried out_by the beast and the world government.

Presently, Christ is in "waiting" mode while mediating sins until the devil is completely released onto the earth. Passages such as Acts 2:34-35 and Hebrews 10:12-13 are based upon the "footstool" reference from Psalm 110 that describes Christ's current position. 1 Corinthians 15:21-26 explains more about this concept that is related to the end times.

> *For as by a man came death, by a man has come also the resurrection of the dead. For as in Adam all die, so also in Christ shall all be made alive. But each in his own order: Christ the firstfruits, then at his coming those who belong to Christ. Then comes the end, when he delivers the kingdom to God the Father after destroying every rule and every authority and power. For he must reign until he has put all his enemies under his feet. The last enemy to be destroyed is death.*

Christ, being Lord over all kings of the earth today (Revelation 1:5), never stated that He has already fulfilled peace on earth (Matthew 10:34). He has obtained complete authority to rule and has the keys to the realm of the dead (Revelation 1:18), but He is in charge of the timing to release the resting saints. According to Paul, death has not yet been destroyed. Furthermore, Christ is not yet ruling with the rod of iron, as mentioned in Psalm 2:7-9. This rod will come out at the second advent that is prophesied in Revelation 19:15 –

*From his mouth comes a sharp sword with which to strike down the nations, and he will rule them with a rod of iron. He will tread the winepress of the fury of the wrath of God the Almighty.*

Peace on earth is to come at the beginning of the next age. Revelation chapters 20-22 depict peace on earth when Christs delivers the heavenly kingdom after defeating all enemies. The devil has been given certain authority until New Jerusalem comes from Heaven (Revelation 21:2-3). Until then, Christ is waiting for the "proper time" (1 Timothy 6:13-16). His kingdom on earth begins at the 7th trumpet that is concurrent with the 2nd advent.

Revelation 11:15 *Then the seventh angel blew his trumpet, and there were loud voices in heaven, saying,* **'The kingdom of the world has become the kingdom of our Lord** *and of his Christ, and he shall reign forever and ever.'*

Christ has all authority in Heaven and on earth (Matthew 28:18 and Ephesians 1:20-23), but He allows the devil to continue reigning over the earthly realm until the set time. The earthly, physical reign of Christ will be announced at the 7th trumpet with the mystery of God being revealed (Revelation 10:7). This is when He comes to earth and cleanses it.

## Timing is in God's Hands

*Acts 1:6 He [Christ] said to them, "It is not for you to know times or seasons that the Father has fixed by his own authority."*

*Matthew 24:36 But concerning that day and hour no one knows [can perceive], not even the angels of heaven, nor the Son, but the Father only.*

Now that we have briefly examined God's authority and control over timing, we should be reminded that there is someone or something holding back the execution of His plan for the end of the age. It is the "Restrainer" that is preventing the antichrist from being revealed.

*2 Thessalonians 2:6 And you know what is restraining him [antichrist] now so that he may be revealed in his time.*

God has always been in control, as only He can allow the antichrist to rise. These three passages describe this period of God's authority as He releases end-time events – Daniel 12:1, 2 Thessalonians 2:6-7 and Revelation 12:7-9.

The archangel Michael helps carry out God's plan to banish the devil from the heavenly realm because the beast system will be authorized to rise on earth once again in its entirety. These developments allow the antichrist to enter the world's scene. There will be a rapid chain of events occurring after God's final countdown begins with the devil's release.

## The Little Horn of Daniel is the Antichrist

Now we will examine the background passages about the antichrist before trying to figure out all the references in the Book of Revelation. He is first described as the little horn that comes out of the last stage of the devil's beast system. We start with the first mention of this most evil person in Daniel chapter 7 verse 8.

> *I considered the horns [of the final beast], and behold, there came up among them another horn [antichrist], a little one... And behold, in this horn were eyes like the eyes of a man, and **a mouth speaking great things**.*

The most important aspect to consider about this verse is that he "speaks great things." This is part of the future Abomination of Desolation that Christ mentioned in Matthew 24 and Paul described in 2 Thessalonians 2.

Daniel 7 provides us with many details about the antichrist that Christ does not repeat in Matthew 24. This is because Christ implies we are to read and understand Daniel. Verse 11 of Daniel 7 states,

> *I looked then because of the sound of the **great words** that the horn [antichrist] was speaking. And as I looked, the beast was killed, and its body destroyed and given over to be burned with fire...*

The timing of the antichrist is during the last days of this age. It is at the time of humanity's last traditional government being abolished when the prostitute system is destroyed (Revelation 17:16). The antichrist rises during this period to establish the devil's governmental and religious system.

The antichrist is granted authority and allowed to conquer the saints for a short time (Revelation 13:7). This is the Great Tribulation Period.

> Daniel 7:21-22 *As I looked, this horn [antichrist] made war with the saints and prevailed over them, until the Ancient of Days came [the 2nd advent], and judgment was given for the saints of the Most High, and the time came when the saints possessed the kingdom.*

The events of <u>Revelation 12:7-12</u> depict when the devil is granted to reveal his power publicly as the antichrist. These passages are at the same time – <u>Daniel 7:25</u> ~ <u>Daniel 12:1</u> ~ <u>Revelation 3:10</u> ~ <u>Revelation 13:7</u>

While Daniel's text seems like it rests on no firm temporal foundation, we can look closely and find enough clues to associate the timing and attributes of these symbols to actual events. We need to correlate prophecies to find overarching themes. God wants us to read the entire Bible to understand His plans.

Daniel 7 verse 20 states that the little horn is *"greater than [his] companions"* of the ten horns. Revelation 17 verse 12 also describes ten horns. These are the *"ten kings who have not yet received royal power"* after the time when John wrote Revelation. From the two verses, we know that the 10 kings and the antichrist are contemporaneous to each other beyond the first century.

## Parallels of Daniel 7 and Revelation 13

The antichrist is described in both chapters with these same identifiers –

√ He comes out of the great beast with 10 horns
√ He speaks complete blasphemy against God

217

✓ He is allowed authority to war over the saints in the tribulation period

✓ He is destroyed at the second coming of Christ (Revelation 17:14)

Daniel 7 verses 24 through 26 conclude the chapter with related descriptions of the antichrist.

Please see the Appendix 8 for a comparison table of passages.

Christ summarizes Daniel's prophecies about the antichrist in one brief passage that begins with verse 15 of Matthew 24.

> *So when you see the abomination of desolation spoken of by the prophet Daniel, standing in the holy place (let the reader understand)*

Christ does not provide details in the following verses of Matthew 24. He expects us to incorporate key prophecies of Daniel chapters 7-12, which speak about a previous abomination that is a foreshadow and the final abomination of the last days.

We studied the Abomination of Desolation in Chapter 21, but it is worth repeating the highlight by Paul. He explains this event when he depicts the antichrist being revealed before the great Day of the Lord.

*2 Thessalonians 2:3-4 Let no one deceive you in any way. For that day will not come, unless the rebellion comes first, and the man of lawlessness is revealed, the son of destruction, who opposes and exalts himself against every so-called god or object of worship, so that he takes his seat in the temple of God, proclaiming himself to be God.*

Paul sheds light on the same abomination that Daniel and Christ spoke about. We should keep in mind the clear meaning of the great words and boasting of the antichrist. He will proclaim to be god. This kicks off the greatest trial even known.

Paul states that the antichrist will take his "seat" in the temple of God, while Christ states he will "stand" in the holy place. This is the same concept using different metaphors. The bottom line is that there will be a great rebellion against God in the Church, in Israel, and all throughout the nations of the earth. This is also the time that false religions are cut off (Revelation 17:16). It is not only that sacrifices of the Jews are affected, or that the Church has a falling away. The entire earth will be distressed (Revelation 13:7).

> *Matthew 24:21-24 For then there will be great tribulation, such as has not been from the beginning of the world until now, no, and never will be. And if those days had not been cut short, no human being would be saved. But for the sake of the elect those days will be cut short. Then if anyone says to you, 'Look, here is the Christ!' or 'There he is!' do not believe it. For false christs and false prophets will arise and perform great signs and wonders, so as to lead astray, if possible, even the elect.*

We can correlate all the abomination passages where the antichrist speaks "great things." We find he exalts himself as god and sets up the final false system of lies.

Daniel 7:8,11,25 = Matthew 24:15-27 = 2 Thessalonians 2:3-4 = Revelation 13 verses 5 and 6 –

> *And the beast was given a mouth uttering haughty and blasphemous words, and it was allowed to exercise authority for forty-two months. It opened its mouth to utter blasphemies against God, blaspheming his name...*

The timing of the antichrist is the 3.5 year (42 months) Great Tribulation Period. All the passages from Daniel and Revelation match each other with the same amount of time. This occurs at the mid-point of Daniels' reported vision of the 70 weeks prophecy. We will study this in Chapter 33.

Later in the Chapter 13, there is a symbol of another beast who differs from the "mouth" coming out of the first beast. There are also similarities. The antichrist and the second beast speak for the first beast (speak like the devil), so they have the same result, since they are both granted authority by the devil. Their combined message spreads and has a dominant influence on the entire earth.

> Revelation 13:11-12 *Then I saw another beast rising out of the earth. It had two horns like a lamb and it spoke like a dragon. It exercises all the authority of the first beast in its presence...*

We notice a difference between the beast that rises from the sea (Daniel 7:3 and Revelation 13:1) compared to the second beast rising from the land. The metaphorical location of the land reveals that the false prophets and false leaders are from mankind and come from the earth like Adam. The first beast is further stated to rise from the spiritual realm out of the pit of death (Revelation 11:7 and Revelation 17:8). These location terms lead us to consider their meanings.

When first beast rises from death (the abyss), described as the pit, it also has a spiritual connection to the nations of the earth described as the sea (Revelation 13:1). However, it is the same primary beast, although at first glance it seems to come from two different locations. The beast comes from the realm of the dead and from the call of the nations for a savior. Their prayers are answered by the emergence of the antichrist. There is a brief party at first, very brief.

> Revelation 11:7-10 *And when they [two witnesses] have finished their testimony, the beast that rises from the bottomless pit will make war on them and conquer them and kill them,... and those who dwell on the earth will rejoice over them and make merry and exchange presents, because these two prophets had been a torment to those who dwell on the earth.*

After it rises, there is a connection of this first beast giving its authority to the second beast of the earth (Revelation 13:12).

The transfer of power shifts from the evil spirit realm to the people of the earth. A large group of followers are enlisted, not just the antichrist being in allegiance with the devil.

Knowing the susceptibility of temptation and gullibility of those who would fall for false signs, we conceptualize that the entire earth will move toward following the devil, except for those with names written in the book of life (Revelation 13:8).

The antichrist will be a man, but will be the spokesperson of the first beast (Daniel 7:8). He will become devil possessed, or a conduit. This person will amplify the end-time program into full motion so it can expand throughout the earth. The beast (devil's spirit) will speak through this person with all power and authority. Revelation 13:5 describes the channeling effect of the devil through the antichrist. Paul also makes it very clear for us to understand the relationship of the antichrist with the devil's spirit.

> The one working behind the curtain is described in 2 Thessalonians 2:9 *The coming of the **lawless one** [antichrist] **is by** the **activity of Satan** with all power and false signs and wonders.*

There are singular and plural nouns that describe channelers of the devil during the Great Tribulation Period. There is one male who is the antichrist, and there are many false prophets and false leaders.

> Matthew 24:24 *For false christs and false prophets will arise and perform great signs and wonders, so as to lead astray, if possible, even the elect.*

The antichrist will rise after the beast emerges, then others will follow him. This is the great rebellion that will envelop the earth. We need to consider the related terms to see the effects. One is that he will be "revealed." This is associated with the rising term we have studied.

We see this term used three times in 2 Thessalonians 2 for the antichrist (a.k.a. the little horn, the man of sin). The uprising is linked to the timing of the revelation of the antichrist.

> 2 Thessalonians 2:3 *Let no one deceive you in any way. For that day will not come, unless **the rebellion comes first**, and **the man of lawlessness is revealed**, the son of destruction.*
>
> 2 Thessalonians 2:6 *And you know what is restraining him now so that **he may be revealed** in his time.*
>
> 2 Thessalonians 2:8 *And then **the lawless one will be revealed**, whom the Lord Jesus will kill with the breath of his mouth and bring to nothing by the appearance of his coming.*

We know similar terms are used in this case, such as Christ warning us about "seeing" the Abomination of Desolation. The revelation of the antichrist occurs visually and audibly. Examples are in the passages about the mouth that speaks "great things" and about visual acts of "signs and wonders." The antichrist and the beast's followers will tell lies and produce false miracles, as shown in Matthew 24:24, 2 Thessalonians 2:9 and Revelation 13:13-15.

We already know that religion and government are affected by the devil's system, and we are also told that it will affect the most basic transactions of every person. Religions and governments differ around the globe now, but they will be reduced toward a single system of one religion and one government that will include a required trade exchange system.

## The Mark of the Beast

This brings us to the Mark of the Beast and how it relates to the antichrist and the coming world system.

> Revelation 13:16-17 *Also it causes all, both small and great, both rich and poor, both free and slave, to be marked on the right hand or the forehead, so that no one can buy or sell unless he has the mark, that is, the name of the beast or the number of its name.*

Many people have tried to figure out the mark of the beast, or if the antichrist is Nero or the return of Nimrod, or some other famous figure. We may have missed the details given to us and the matching symbolic language. The mark of the beast and the antichrist are great beacons of the warnings for all humanity. These warnings are crucial for us to understand.

Is the Mark of the Beast the number of man, or *a* man? Revelation 13:18 states,

> *This calls for wisdom: let the one who has understanding calculate the number of the beast, for it is the number of **a man**, and his number is 666.*

In most other English passages, this exact Greek phrase translates as "of man," not "of a man." The root word can refer to an individual or mankind. Within the context, we should consider that all humanity is affected by the devil's spiritual influence. The beast's number means mankind in our interpretation, not an individual man's number like the antichrist. Humanity will enter an alliance with the beast system to control religion, government, and trade.

The key figure of the Great Tribulation Period is the devil, not the antichrist. His target is humanity. The primary focus of this period is that God will use the devil to test the entire earth. For that reason, humanity will go through the greatest refinement of all time (Jeremiah 9:7, Daniel 11:35, Malachi 3:2).

It is of utmost importance that we remember God cares about saving as many people as possible (Romans 9:22-23, 1 Timothy 2:4, 2 Peter 3:3-9).

*Ezekiel 18:23 Have I any pleasure in the death of the wicked, declares the Lord GOD, and not rather that he should turn from his way and live?*

The tribulation days are "cut short" (Mathew 24:22) by God to save the remnant of the world (Isaiah 10:20-23 and Isaiah 66:18-21). The Day of the Lord is mentioned in Matthew 24:29-30 and the 6th seal of Revelation Chapter 6 to bring an end to the greatest tribulation of all time. The second advent occurs at the end of the Day of the Lord period to save the righteous and the survivors of the nations.

*Romans 9:27-28 And Isaiah cries out concerning Israel: "Though the number of the sons of Israel be as the sand of the sea, only a remnant of them will be saved, for the Lord will carry out his sentence upon the earth fully and without delay."*

We find interesting associations in these passages about the last days of those who do not repent to those who believe in lies –

2 Thessalonians 2:10b *they refused to love the truth and so be saved.*

Daniel 12:10b *but the wicked shall act wickedly. And none of the wicked shall understand, but those who are wise shall understand.*

2 Timothy 3:1-2a *But understand this, that in the last days there will come times of difficulty. For people will be lovers of self.*

When considering all related Scripture passages, we see that the antichrist, together with other false messiahs and prophets, are leaders in the rebellion. God's primary concern is found in the warnings to average people not to follow the path mapped out to the devil by these leaders.

The last details about the antichrist are prophesied in Revelation 19:19-20. Daniel 7:11,22,26 and 2 Thessalonians 2:8. These passages are the same event that occurs at the end of the battle of Armageddon. It is the start of Christ's earthly kingdom as He takes over the earth. The antichrist will only realize a moment of fame, then the world will see his true colors.

*Revelation 19:20 And the beast was captured, and with it the false prophet who in its presence had done the signs by which he deceived those who had received the mark of the beast and those who worshiped its image. These two were thrown alive into the lake of fire that burns with sulfur.*

The term to be thrown "alive" into the lake of fire relates to the beast that takes its final earthly form in the antichrist's body. Daniel equated the little horn coming out of the final beast as its personification. The antichrist and the devil's spirit become one after the Restrainer allows the "big reveal."

*Daniel 7:11 I looked then because of the sound of the great words that the horn was speaking. And as I looked, the beast was killed, and its body destroyed and given over to be burned with fire.*

## Summary of the Antichrist

The beast that rises in the last days is the devil's spiritual reign over earth, beginning with the person of the antichrist.

The antichrist will be part of the 10 kings (horns of Daniel 7:24) of the global system run by mankind before the devil enters the scene.

The 10 horns are the 7th head of the beast (Revelation 17:9-11), not the completed beast.

The antichrist will become possessed by the devil's spirit as he rises out of the 10 global kingdoms to take control and form the completed 8th head of the beast (Revelation 17:11).

There will be one world government at that time, but not controlled by mankind. All leaders of the world will hand over their power to the world system of the beast (Revelation 17:13).

This beast's final form of the antichrist will be destroyed by Christ (Revelation 17:14 and Revelation 19:19-20). However, the devil himself, as an angelic being, will live on for a little while longer, according to God's plan (Revelation 20:1-4).

The beast will come up from the abyss for one last hurrah as the antichrist. However, it will never again have any spiritual influence over mankind's governmental or religious systems once Christ sets up His eternal kingdom.

> Zechariah 14:9 *And the LORD will be king over all the earth. On that day the LORD will be one and his name one.*

<u>2 Thessalonians 1:5-10</u> *This is evidence of the righteous judgment of God, that you may be considered worthy of the kingdom of God, for which you are also suffering— since indeed God considers it just to repay with affliction those who afflict you, and to grant relief to you who are afflicted as well as to us, when the Lord Jesus is revealed from heaven with his mighty angels in flaming fire, inflicting vengeance on those who do not know God and on those who do not obey the gospel of our Lord Jesus. They will suffer the punishment of eternal destruction, away from the presence of the Lord and from the glory of his might, when he comes on that day to be glorified in his saints, and to be marveled at among all who have believed, because our testimony to you was believed.*

# Chapter 30

*Who Is the False Prophet of Revelation?*

## The Spread of the Beast's System

The False Prophet is the most important concept to understand in the Book of Revelation besides the Day of the Lord, culminating with the second advent of Christ. There are no greater warnings issued for us to be aware of than those that are related to the False Prophet. If you think the antichrist is the most important villain in Revelation, you will be surprised to find out why he is not. The False Prophet is certainly underrated, so it is understandable that the antichrist gets all the attention.

Let's look at what the book of Revelation revolves around. There's the true second coming of Christ that is delayed, and then there's the counterfeit message of the false messiah as the second coming that comes first. The False Prophet is the symbol of those most responsible for delivering this message.

Revelation resonates with us most deeply because of its illuminating focus on salvation. However, there is a true version observed from interpreting the symbols of the heavenly realm, and a false version with the attempts by humanity to save itself by believing the lies of the beast's deceptive means. We will see how the devil will promote this false agenda, which is linked to the greatest test in human history.

Many Bible students focus on the beast, its mark, or the antichrist. However, as we have shown in previous chapters, the antichrist as the beast on earth is not prophesied with the most prominent warnings to test humanity.

## Testing of the Great Tribulation Period

Before diving into the details of the False Prophet, we should investigate God's purpose for testing humankind. God does not tempt anyone (James 1:12-15), but He certainly tests us.

Please review these passages about testing – Job 23:10-14; Psalm 7:9; Isaiah 48:9-11; Jeremiah 9:7, 11:19-20; Zechariah 13:7-9; Luke 8:11-15; 1 Corinthians 3:13; 1 Thessalonians 2:4; Hebrews 3:8; James 1:12; 1 Peter 1:7, 4:12.

There are analogies about animals like sheep that are often used to explain God's plan of testing. It does not seem like God has a high opinion of us at first. Our current condition, like the analogy of animals, should be differentiated from our future state when we are made perfect at the resurrection of the dead (Philippians 3:10-21).

Ecclesiastes 3:18 *I said in my heart with regard to the children of man that God is testing them that they may see that they themselves are but beasts [animals].*

Isaiah 53:6a *All we like sheep have gone astray; we have turned—every one—to his own way;*

Jeremiah 12:3 *But you, O LORD, know me; you see me, and test my heart toward you. Pull them out like sheep for the slaughter, and set them apart for the day of slaughter.*

Romans 8:35-37 *Who shall separate us from the love of Christ? Shall tribulation, or distress, or persecution, or famine, or nakedness, or danger, or sword? As it is written,*

*"For your sake we are being killed all the day long; we are regarded as sheep to be slaughtered." No, in all these things we are more than conquerors through him who loved us.*

Does God want destruction or great suffering? No. They must be necessary if He does not take pleasure in punishing creation for rejecting Him. Some do not answer His call.

Isaiah 65:12 *I will destine you to the sword, and all of you shall bow down to the slaughter, because, when I called, you did not answer; when I spoke, you did not listen, but you did what was evil in my eyes and chose what I did not delight in.*

2 Peter 3:9 *The Lord is not slow to fulfill his promise as some count slowness, but is patient toward you, not wishing that any should perish, but that all should reach repentance.*

These passages provide background to learn about the nature of God and His reasoning behind judgment. It will be the end of the age when God allows the entire earth to go through tribulation to accomplish the final part of His plan for redemption. We do not fully understand why God would test people with such extreme measures. Apparently, great tribulation will be the method He uses to bring our attention toward His righteous judgment on the earth. Most likely, the Church will become even more complacent than it is now. We forget about God when life is easy. This requires the biggest wake-up call ever heard.

> Genesis 3:17 *And to Adam he said, "Because you have listened to the voice of your wife and have eaten of the tree of which I commanded you, 'You shall not eat of it,' cursed is the ground because of you;* **in pain** *you shall eat of it all the days of your life;"*

The beginning and end of the age of man starts with pain and ends with pain. The next passages speak of the Great Tribulation Period.

> Matthew 24:8 *All these are but the beginning of the birth* **pains**.

> 1 Thessalonians 5:3 *While people are saying, "There is peace and security," then sudden destruction will come upon them as labor* **pains** *come upon a pregnant woman, and they will not escape.*

There is good news! Paul summarizes for us the reason behind the suffering of God's creation. Romans 8:18-23 –

*For I consider that the sufferings of this present time are not worth comparing with the glory that is to be revealed to us. For the creation waits with eager longing for the revealing of the sons of God. For the creation was subjected to futility, not willingly, but because of him who subjected it, in hope that the creation itself will be set free from its bondage to corruption and obtain the freedom of the glory of the children of God. For we know that the whole creation has been groaning together in the pains of childbirth until now. And not only the creation, but we ourselves, who have the firstfruits of the Spirit, groan inwardly as we wait eagerly for adoption as sons, the redemption of our bodies.*

The greatest test of our age is shown by Christ to be part of the Great Tribulation Period. After examining all other passages about testing, we can conclude that the Great Tribulation Period and the great hour of testing are directly related. They occur at the same time. Why would Christ issue so many warnings if believers are not to experience some form of tribulation? Some people will receive divine protection, but not everyone.

> Matthew 24:21 *For then there will be great tribulation, such as has not been from the beginning of the world until now, no, and never will be.*
>
> Revelation 3:10 *Because you have kept my word about patient endurance, I will keep you from* **the hour of trial that is coming on the whole world**, *to try those who dwell on the earth*

Now, we come to the most important advice for the end of this age. It can be found in Revelation 13:9-10. There are only two options for believers mentioned in this solemn passage.

> *If anyone has an ear, let him hear:*
> *If anyone is to be* **taken captive**,
> *to captivity he goes;*
> *if anyone is to be* **slain with the sword**,
> *with the sword must he be slain.*
> *Here is a call for the endurance*
> *and faith of the saints.*

This advice is written to the believers who will go through tribulation, not the wrath of God. This passage is in the middle of Revelation 13 where God allows the beast, antichrist, and false prophets to bring great distress upon the saints. See Revelation 13:5-15.

238

Why does God allow the devil to have such power during this awful time? It is the same answer as any other period in history, that His mercy will be magnified (see Romans 9:14-24 and Romans 11:30-33). He uses leaders of the earth to carry out His will.

> Revelation 17:17 *for God has put it into their hearts to carry out **his purpose** by being of one mind and handing over their royal power to the beast, until the words of God are fulfilled.*

There are only a few options for believers during the Great Tribulation Period. One is not mentioned in Revelation 13. It relates to the 144,000 who are sealed (Revelation 7:3, 9:4) and those who are protected by God (carried on eagle's wings of Revelation 12:14). The other group that goes through persecution of the tribulation period is of the woman's offspring where the devil seeks to destroy them (Revelation 12:17, Revelation 13:7).

One part of the persecuted offspring group found in Revelation 13:9 will be taken captive. They will not accept the message of the false prophets and will be restricted from buying and selling. Captives will pass God's test of tribulation, where faith is tested (1 Peter 1:7).

The other persecuted group will be martyred, as described in Revelation 13:10. This is referenced several times in the book of Revelation. It is the highest honor bestowed by God for passing His test. See Revelation 2:10, Revelation 6:9-11, Revelation 14:12-13, Revelation 17:6, Revelation 20:4-6.

We will find comfort and rewards for going through this difficult period (if we do not follow the beast). There are other passages that describe persecution as something to be expected, whether in the tribulation period or at any time.

*Matthew 5:11-12 Blessed are you when others revile you and persecute you and utter all kinds of evil against you falsely on my account. Rejoice and be glad, for your reward is great in heaven, for so they persecuted the prophets who were before you.*

*Matthew 16:24-26 Then Jesus told his disciples, "If anyone would come after me, let him deny himself and take up his cross and follow me. For whoever would save his life will lose it, but whoever loses his life for my sake will find it. For what will it profit a man if he gains the whole world and forfeits his soul? Or what shall a man give in return for his soul?"*

*Matthew 24:9 Then they will deliver you up to tribulation and put you to death, and you will be hated by all nations for my name's sake.*

*James 1:12 Blessed is the man who remains steadfast under trial, for when he has stood the test he will receive the crown of life, which God has promised to those who love him.*

## Who Is the False Prophet?

Now that we have foreseen the importance of the trials and tribulation in the last days, we can learn about the role of the False Prophet, a key figure who stands as one of our chief antagonists and the one responsible for the downfall of many. The relationship of the False Prophet to the greatest testing period becomes clear.

We begin with a review of the passages about the False Prophet. There are only two sections in Revelation. We know the second beast of Revelation 13 is the False Prophet symbol. Revelation 19:20 summarizes the same entity in Revelation 13:11-16.

Revelation 13:11-18 *Then I saw another beast rising out of the earth. It had two horns like a lamb and it spoke like a dragon. It exercises all the authority of the first beast in its presence, and makes the earth and its inhabitants worship the first beast, whose mortal wound was healed. It performs great signs, even making fire come down from heaven to earth in front of people, and by the signs that it is allowed to work in the presence of the beast it deceives those who dwell on earth, telling them to make an image for the beast that was wounded by the sword and yet lived. And it was allowed to give breath to the image of the beast, so that the image of the beast might even speak and might cause those who would not worship the image of the beast to be slain. Also it causes all, both small and great, both rich and poor, both free and slave, to be marked on the right hand or the forehead, so that no one can buy or sell unless he has the mark, that is, the name of the beast or the number of its name. This calls for wisdom: let the one who has understanding calculate the number of the beast, for it is the number of a man, and his number is 666.*

We first need to notice that there is not one false prophet, but many. The book of Revelation is packed with symbolism, but it is easy to behold the meaning. The False Prophet is a symbol of the widespread movement of numerous people against God. We know this from Matthew 24:23-26 –

> Then if anyone says to you, 'Look, here is the Christ!' or 'There he is!' do not believe it. For **false christs** and **false prophets** will arise and **perform great signs and wonders**, so as to lead astray, if possible, even the elect. See, I have told you beforehand. So, if they say to you, 'Look, he is in the wilderness,' do not go out. If they say, 'Look, he is in the inner rooms,' do not believe it.

Another key phrase to consider about the connection of the false prophets in Matthew 24 is related to "signs and wonders." These terms are repeated in Revelation 13:13-14 and are also corroborated in 2 Thessalonians 2:9 –

> The coming of the lawless one is by the activity of Satan with all power and false signs and wonders,

We learn from examining 2 Thessalonians 2, Revelation 13, and together with Revelation 16, that the ability to perform signs comes from the devil and the demonic realm. Human false prophets are connected to this realm. We notice in this next verse that demonic spirits do not perform the main act of work, it is people who carry out the work of demons.

> Revelation 16:14 *For they are demonic spirits, performing signs, who go abroad to the kings of the whole world, to assemble them for battle on the great day of God the Almighty.*

The activity of the devil and the demonic realm reminds us of Genesis 6 and other passages we studied in the "Who Are the Sons of God in Genesis 6?" chapter. There has been and will be authority granted by the devil passed through the demonic realm to humans. These false prophets and messiahs are possessed by demons. Demons need a host body to deploy the work of the devil in a similar way that God uses believers to carry out his good works through the power of the Holy Spirit.

We find that there will be many people involved to carry out end-time events. The person of the antichrist will not perform most of the work during the tribulation period. Instead, the antichrist leads by example to show all people of the earth how to rebel against God in the highest form, to claim independence from God. There will be a culture shift with peer pressure involved as demonic influence increases to gain more followers.

## What Is the Role of the False Prophet?

Rather than simply rising up from out of nowhere, the false prophet's rise to power occurs because of a chain of authority we need to recognize. Let's learn how the false prophets arise and how their message will affect the average person during the Great Tribulation Period. Many of us take comfort in our beliefs and feel we have nothing to fear, but what about when we are tested beyond anything we have experienced? Should we wait to see what happens or be prepared?

God has complete control over creation, yet He allows the devil to have power over the earth for a brief period of great deception (2 Thessalonians 2:11, Revelation 12:12-13). The devil is cast from heaven at the same time his beast spirit rises from the pit. He "stands" over the people of the earth when this occurs (Revelation 12:17-13:1).

The devil's authority is transferred through his spirit to the antichrist (2 Thessalonians 2:9, Revelation 13:1-8). This is because the devil does not come to earth in his own bodily form (i.e., the dragon being thrown to earth is a symbol). He works through the spirit realm of the beast where he has worked from since the fall, but he will have a body next time, like he had in the Garden of Eden.

The earthly leaders of the end times also grant their authority to the beast system (Revelation 17:12-13). God allows this through His divine will (Revelation 17:17).

Finally, we see authority exercised by the false prophets after this chain of command is developed. There is a differentiation between their authority and the authority granted to the antichrist. The antichrist receives direct authority, primarily for political power to enforce the system, where the false prophets have indirect authority granted through the demonic realm of the beast.

> Revelation 13:12a *It [false prophets] exercises all the authority of the first beast **in its presence**, and makes the earth and its inhabitants worship the first beast*

The false prophets can only carry out the plan of the devil through interaction with the spirit realm. This is demonic "presence" and relates to the image of the beast we will examine later. Another key statement in this verse is that they "make" the earth worship the demonic realm.

## Summary of Authority Granted to the False Prophet

God's sovereignty > grants temporary authority to the devil > the devil channels all his authority through his spirit > the antichrist assumes the devil's spirit when the beast rises from the pit > the false prophets are allowed to exercise authority under the influence of the beast > this chain leads to deception and control of individuals.

The antichrist is one person, while demons cannot do anything without a host (person). There must be many people that are part of the great deception of the end times. This is the purpose of false prophets.

They are the ones who will have the greatest impact upon humanity, not the antichrist. It is group force, not individual control that will occur.

There are several duties of false prophets. We observe they carry out most of the work during the Great Tribulation Period.

## The Roles of the False Prophet

- They institute the image of the beast
- They institute the mark of the beast
- They force the people of the earth to be part of the beast system
- They perform signs and wonders by deception to enable their power

This summary is also explained by a word study shown in Appendix 9.

# What Are the Signs and Wonders of the False Prophets?

We have already shown that Matthew 24 connects the false prophets to the False Prophet symbol of Revelation. What is their detailed job description? It is important to understand because they are the impetus to convince the world to take the Mark of the Beast.

There are means of deception used to lead people astray from God when the initial thrust of enforcement begins. This is a common pattern we notice about the tribulation period before the Mark is instituted. Christ mentioned this deception several times in Matthew 24:4-5, 24:11, and 24:24.

As we have shown earlier, the pattern of leading people astray through signs is repeated in Revelation 13:13-14 and 2 Thessalonians 2:9. The chain of events we are looking for will be found after we see that the signs and wonders lead to the use of force. The Mark of the Beast and people getting killed are warning signs, but believers will have long recognized that these occurrences are part of the plan that has been in motion for a considerable time.

When we consider Revelation 13:13a again, we should realize this connection.

> *and by the signs... it [false prophet] deceives those who dwell on earth*

We know the signs are not true power, even though they will be convincing. Fire coming down from the heavens mentioned in verse 13 is a "false" sign to deceive people. There needs to be a sense of great power established through these signs so that people will take the Mark.

What looks like signs and wonders are actually the means that enable false prophets to engage in a global use of force. Earlier in Revelation 13, we get another sense of the great deception and power that it brings.

> Revelation 13:3b-4 **the whole earth marveled** *as they followed the beast. And they worshiped the dragon, for he had given his authority to the beast, and they worshiped the beast, saying, "Who is like the beast, and* **who can fight against it?"**

The term "marveled" is linked to signs and wonders. However, the perception of inability to fight against the beast demonstrates a belief in its unbeatable power from the signs.

Only Christ can fight the beast and false prophets. We do not need to use force.

> Revelation 19:19-20a *And I saw the beast and the kings of the earth with their armies gathered to make war against him [Christ] who was sitting on the horse and against his army. And the beast was captured, and with it the false prophet who in its presence had done the signs by which he deceived those who had received the mark of the beast and those who worshiped its image.*

## Will the False Prophet Force People to Worship the Devil?

The concept of force is strong persuasion to "convince" people to do something. We should realize that most people will probably not worship the beast because they love the devil. They will be *compelled* to bow down, while believers will go into captivity or to death after resisting these forceful methods.

Please remember that the greatest test of humanity occurs during the Great Tribulation Period. This test is for believers, but also to judge unbelievers that assume the image of the beast. The same judgment period accomplishes two distinct purposes of God.

It is very interesting that God can harden people's hearts like a pharaoh or an unbeliever. The person must remain in rejection of God before He will let them take the Mark of the Beast. We see this described in 2 Thessalonians 2:9-12 –

> *The coming of the lawless one is by the activity of Satan with all power and false signs and wonders, and with all wicked deception for those who are perishing, because* **they refused to love the truth and so be saved**. *Therefore God sends them a strong delusion, so that they may believe what is false, in order that all may be condemned who did not believe the truth but had pleasure in unrighteousness.*

Revelation 14:6-7 reports that the gospel will be given to the entire earth until the end. This is to show God's fairness that He presents every opportunity, but many will refuse.

People who follow the beast will not repent during the Day of the Lord that occurs at the end of the Great Tribulation Period. See Revelation 9:20-21 and Revelation 16:8-11. They will reject God before these final events occur. Then their hearts will be hardened.

Lawlessness against God is the main theme of humanity during the end times. This is rebellion. Sin prevailing over the earth is mentioned in more warnings than taking the Mark or any other participation with the devil, the beast or the antichrist. The false prophets are the majority that cause sin and rebellion. The antichrist leads by example.

These passages speak about the unrighteous people living in the tribulation period of the great deception, the final rebellion.

> Daniel 12:10b *the wicked shall act wickedly. And none of the wicked shall understand, but those who are wise shall understand.*
>
> Matthew 24:12 *And because lawlessness will be increased, the love of many will grow cold.*
>
> 2 Thessalonians 2:3 *Let no one deceive you in any way. For that day will not come, unless the rebellion comes first, and the man of lawlessness is revealed, the son of destruction,*

Worshipping the devil is the base sin of selfishness. There is no need to bow down directly and praise him. People who follow his ways are *like* him. This is in part the image of the beast, the sin of pride that magnifies throughout all the earth. The greatest rebellion ever will occur when lawlessness is increased. The earth will defy God!

## What Is the Image of the Beast?

We are ready to investigate the purpose of the image of the beast. The false prophets are the ones who bring the image into view. Why is there an indirect method or reflection needed since we often think about direct influence of the antichrist?

The image of the beast is created by spirit. The Greek root word for breath is the same as spirit (pneuma). This means that the image of the beast comes from the evil spirit realm.

> Revelation 13:15 *And it was allowed to give* **breath [spirit]** *to the image of the beast, so that the image of the beast might even speak and might cause those who would not worship the image of the beast to be slain.*

We find that the image of the beast and its Mark are part of the same movement. This relationship is found in verses 15 and 16.

The image "causes" the Mark of the Beast.

Revelation 13:16 *Also it [the image] causes all, both small and great, both rich and poor, both free and slave, to be marked on the right hand or the forehead,*

It is most important to know that it is not the devil, or the antichrist, who implements the Mark upon the earth. It is the image of the beast that "brands" the Mark, which we know comes directly from spiritual influence through the false prophets.

This leads us to the supreme theme of all Revelation memes about evil. The image of the beast is people. The spirit of humanity will embrace deception and spread it to others.

The first thing that came to my mind when I heard this concept was Charlton Heston's warning about Soylent Green. After this thought faded, I realized that Revelation 13 is the greatest warning of the end times. Revelation was given to us for hope and to caution everyone not to perform any action to "be like God" (Genesis 3:5). It is my prayer that this also helps you to prepare for the greatest deception of the coming last days.

We should realize that there are two ways the image of the beast and its Mark are carried out. One is a direct approach to claim godhood. This is related to the name of the beast, something we'll be investigating further. The other way is related to the number of the beast that is indirect worship of the beast. There will be people acting by self-preservation, instead of relying on the true God unto salvation.

An example of people carrying out the beast's plans through demonic influence can be found by reviewing another section of Revelation 13:15 –

> *And it was allowed to give breath to the image of the beast, so that the* **image of the beast might even speak** *and might cause those who would not worship the image of the beast to be slain.*

It seems strange that the image speaks to cause those who do not worship itself to be slain. Why does the image not reiterate the worship of the devil or the primary beast as referenced in Revelation 13:4? This is probably because of our theory at hand that this passage is about people. The image spreads self-interest and a dire need to seek preservation at all costs. People will convince others to follow the beast, so this message grows into a large force. Will people worship the beast directly or the replicant image? Both, as we shall see, but most worship seems to be the image being replicated.

There is a progression we can follow in Revelation 13 that shows worship of the dragon and the beast mentioned earlier in Revelation to be completed by the message spreading into greater power towards the end of the chapter. The antichrist and the group of 10 kingdoms are focused on political power while the false prophets expand the power into the religious realm of individual lives through demonic possession.

Most people do not want to worship someone else like the antichrist. We connect to false gods so we can get something in return or save our skin. The growth of the image of the beast creates a scenario where the average person agrees with the masses to be "saved" or kept alive during the darkest hours.

Remember, beast worship and image worship are connected to the use of force and peer pressure until they become the same. The passages we have seen about worshipping the beast will result in self-serving interests. The antichrist will lead the way when he claims to be god (Daniel 7:25, Matthew 24:15, 2 Thessalonians 2:4, Revelation 13:5-6), knowing good and evil. Many will follow his lies by making a similar decision, like mankind's belief in the first lie of being like God. The same lie began the age of man and will end our age.

We can expound further with the root word for image, meaning more than a mirror or reflection. It is a *replication* of what the devil does through the antichrist in this case. The opposite is being *made* into the image of God (1 Corinthians 15:49, Colossians 3:10).

There is an initial concept in Revelation 13 of the direct worship of the beast through force, but then worship is explained to have greater power with the Mark and image through strength in numbers.

Multitudes are needed to spread the message of the beast, since pure political power is not enough. The antichrist leads people to the false way of being God (2 Thessalonians 2:4). This is reinforced by the false prophets through the image.

When we boil all these concepts down, there is one fundamental theme that emerges, one that everyone we know has been guilty of at one time or another. It is selfishness. While we all have our selfish moments and have experienced times when we've sinned or given into temptation, human nature's faults are magnified during the end times in ways that we can't truly imagine. The weaknesses of the flesh are exposed in greater detail. People will try to save themselves via allegiance with the beast rather than repent to be saved by grace alone, by faith alone, through Christ alone.

In the end, there will be a spiritual alignment from our earthly realm to God, or the devil. We will be like God, or be like the devil. There is no gray area and there will be no lukewarm believers at the end of this age. All living people will come to the Valley of Decision at that time (Joel 3:14).

## Summary of the False Prophet

- Predetermination of God's will leads to authority granted to the beast.

- The beast, working through the antichrist, end time leaders and false prophets, carries out God's plan to test the earth.
- Authority of the beast begins when the devil's power is removed from the heavenly realm and is solely focused on earth. This occurs simultaneously as the beast rises in the bodily form of the antichrist. He is directly possessed by the devil's spirit.
- The false prophets are granted indirect authority to carry out coercive measures, beginning with the use of signs.
- Signs, marvels, and wonders enable the use of the force by the display of these powers, which in turn greatly impress the people of the earth towards false worship.
- The powers of the world government, aligned with the false prophets, create a great war upon the minds to compel the people of the earth to make a choice.
- The people of the earth come to a bottleneck, where they need to decide to follow the beast system, be martyred, or be sent into captivity.

Please see the Review in <u>Appendix 9</u> for a map to follow these key events found in Revelation 13.

Now we are ready to "calculate" the Mark of the Beast to see if this theory about the image of the beast holds true. Before we continue, please remember that the false prophets are granted authority to create the image, and the image creates the Mark of the Beast.

# Chapter 31

*What Is the Mark of the Beast?*

## The Symbol of 666 Is Explained by the Original Greek Text

The Mark of the Beast that is mentioned in Revelation 13 looms large like a cloud over our discussion of the end times. It's spurred theories, taken shape as an object to fear, and even gained traction as something to reference within popular culture. Of course, many have assumed that the Mark, with its name and number, is associated with the person of the antichrist.

We will consider none of those theories since we are focused on our concept about the image of the beast as being people who will be caught up in its deception and worship themselves. We will explore how the Mark is related to the image.

First, let's examine biblical mentions of marking, whether for believers or unbelievers. After we examine contextual passages, we should be able to determine the Mark of the Beast and its number, 666.

> Revelation 13:18 *This calls for wisdom: let the one who has understanding calculate the number of the beast, for it is the number of a man, and his number is 666.*

We are ready to go back in time to learn about previous markings in Scripture. The first mark we notice is found in Genesis 4:15, where Cain was marked by God to be protected. Marks on the doorposts were also used at the original Passover as a means of protection.

In another account, there is a command given in Exodus 13:15b-16.

> *... all the firstborn of my sons I redeem. It shall be **as a mark** on your hand or frontlets between your eyes, for by a strong hand the LORD brought us out of Egypt.*

The meaning here is that this symbolic mark is like a reminder of something sanctified by God. Israel was commanded to set apart their firstborn so they can remember what the Lord has done. These were not literal marks, like the branding of an animal. The firstborn sons are figurative marks to remind Israel of God's redemption.

There are different meanings and uses of marking as we have seen. Depending on the case, marks are described as literal imprints or metaphorical identifications, for separation or protection. In all these cases, God used marks to segregate people for His purpose. Marks can be physical or spiritual symbols that take on particular relevance according to who is marked.

Sealing is another figurative term like a non-physical marking.

> 2 Corinthians 1:22 *and who has also put his **seal** on us and given us his Spirit in our hearts as a guarantee.*

Now we can look deeper into marking good and evil people. We read of examples in Ezekiel like those in Revelation.

*Chapter 9 ... "Bring near the executioners of the city, each with his destroying weapon in his hand." And behold, six men came from the direction of the upper gate, which faces north, each with his weapon for slaughter in his hand, and with them was a man clothed in linen, with a writing case at his waist.*

*And the LORD said to him, "Pass through the city, through Jerusalem, and put a mark on the foreheads of the men who sigh and groan over all the abominations that are committed in it."*

*And to the others he said in my hearing, "Pass through the city after him, and strike. Your eye shall not spare, and you shall show no pity. Kill old men outright, young men and maidens, little children and women, but touch no one on whom is the mark..."*

*"Ah, Lord GOD! Will you destroy all the remnant of Israel in the outpouring of your wrath on Jerusalem?" ... "As for me, my eye will not spare, nor will I have pity; I will bring their deeds upon their heads."*

There is good news a little later in Ezekiel 11. This is comparable to Revelation where a remnant of the world makes it through the trials of the Great Tribulation Period.

Chapter 11 ... *"Ah, Lord GOD! Will you make a full end of the remnant of Israel?"*

*And the word of the LORD came to me: "Son of man, your brothers, even your brothers, your kinsmen, the whole house of Israel, all of them, are those of whom the inhabitants of Jerusalem have said, 'Go far from the LORD; to us this land is given for a possession.' Therefore say, 'Thus says the Lord GOD: Though I removed them far off among the nations, and though I scattered them among the countries, yet I have been a sanctuary to them for a while in the countries where they have gone.' Therefore say, 'Thus says the Lord GOD: I will gather you from the peoples and assemble you out of the countries where you have been scattered, and I will give you the land of Israel.' And when they come there, they will remove from it all its detestable things and all its abominations. And I will give them one heart, and a new spirit I will put within them. I will remove the heart of stone from their flesh and give them a heart of flesh, that they may walk in my statutes and keep my rules and obey them. And they shall be my people, and I will be their God. But as for those whose heart goes after their detestable things and their abominations, I will bring their deeds upon their own heads, declares the Lord GOD."*

Revelation 7 reports sealing of those who will be protected during the tribulation at the end of this age. An angel says in verse 3,

*"Do not harm the earth or the sea or the trees, until we have sealed the servants of our God on their foreheads."*

This is like the passage we read in Ezekiel 9. God always protects His remnant of believers, whether by marking or sealing. However, He also allows marks to establish the destruction of unbelievers. Marks can be good or bad.

Perhaps the most important aspect to know about marking in the Bible is that it relates to believing and trusting in God (or not) in periods of great judgment. The marks play a critical role in contrasting good and evil. Impending judgment follows markings that identify believers for protection during a judgment period or identify unbelievers for destruction when God's wrath is poured out.

There are certainly a lot of symbols in the Book of Revelation. When we consider the Mark of the Beast from a spiritual perspective, we see people in alignment with the devil through his beast system. There are few convincing arguments from the biblical context that there needs to be a physical mark like a tattoo on people. Ezekiel 9 reports an "invisible" mark that only angels can see. The mark in Revelation could be any identifier that shows allegiance to the beast system. People will know who is a follower of the beast.

Just as with Ezekiel 9, the Mark of the Beast mentioned in Revelation 13 is symbolic. The mark on the hands of unbelievers may signify actions against God, while marks upon foreheads signify conscious decisions that people will make to worship the devil's beast system directly.

There will be direct and indirect worship of the devil by the people during the Great Tribulation Period who will rebel against God. Direct worship is associated with the name of the beast, while indirect worship relates to the number of the beast. It seems that the majority will be part of the number of the beast and follow this system through compelling means of deception. Some people will openly worship the devil's system of the beast, even if they do not think they are worshiping the devil himself. They will probably think the antichrist is a savior at first, not a nemesis.

The main point to consider about markings of this kind is that they are mostly used by angels during periods of judgment to separate people. The end times are certainly a time of judgment upon the earth, so markings would be expected. Angels will know the separation between believers and unbelievers, but what about humanity? What will we physically observe during the Great Tribulation Period?

If we consider the role of the false prophets in Revelation 13, we will connect the image of the beast to its Mark. The Mark is the brand of the image, while the image is people. These people will be identified with the beast system. They will spread the power of the beast through any controls necessary, such as social credits, digital passports or central bank digital currency.

Taking the Mark is to be in allegiance with the devil. It goes beyond buying and selling. God is concerned with sin and lawlessness in all forms. The ability to buy or sell stems from rebellion against God. Most people will not repent.

> Revelation 9:20 *The rest of mankind, who were not killed by these plagues, did not repent of the works of their hands nor give up worshiping demons...*

Being marked on the hands symbolizes the actions of following the beast. Being marked on the head symbolizes direct agreement with the devil's beast system. Those who take the name of the beast are those who have the head mark. These people openly worship the devil or his beast system. The people who are marked on the hands are the same as those counted in the beast's number. They probably account for most people of the end times. They will unintentionally worship the beast by following the rebellion. These people may bow down to the devil's lies without full knowledge.

The false prophets have authority to "make" people worship the devil's system as we notice in Revelation 13.

- *makes the earth and its inhabitants worship the first beast,*

- *cause those who would not worship the image of the beast to be slain.*

- *causes all...to be marked on the right hand or the forehead, so that no one can buy or sell unless he has the mark.*

How do false prophets cause people to follow the beast? Think of a company with morally negligent business practices that you need to purchase from even though you know they do bad things like supporting child slave labor in other countries. Forcing people to buy and sell through a non-optional system created by these false prophets will be a powerful way that they can enforce the Mark. They will eliminate free market competition. People will do almost anything to get what they need to survive in the new society so they will comply with the Mark.

People often rebel against the force of extreme government control, but there may be a more subtle method. It will be easier to "sell" the message if the masses agree in a widespread rebellion that begins with deception. The image of the beast will grow with peer pressure to take the Mark. Large groups may think they are saving lives by signing up for the system, but in fact they will love sin more than truth (Daniel 12:10, 2 Thessalonians 2:9-12).

The impetus for the creation of the mark comes after signs and wonders, not solely by governmental brute force of the antichrist and world government. There will be two areas of focus – the false prophets will have a job to attract the masses, while the government leaders will war against the saints. Believers of the true God will be vilified by all sides, from armies using force to the average person telling the government that their believing neighbor does not comply with the beast system.

Former friends, neighbors, and family members will help send believers to death or captivity. Is this too hard to believe? It has happened before. Some people want to survive more than doing the right thing.

## The Mark of the Beast Explained

What is the Mark of the Beast? We learn the answer from the original Greek as we find by examining Revelation 13:17 ... *the name of the beast or the **number** of its name.*

The name of the beast means open worship of the beast. This is not forced because some people will choose this intentional path. They believe satan's lead, worship of self. The main warning at the end of Revelation 13 is about the number of the beast, not the name. Humanity will rebel against God on a grand scale because of the hint that the number provides.

> let the one who has understanding **calculate** the number of the beast, for it is the **number** of a **man**, and his number is 666.

There are three crucial terms in Revelation 13:18. One is "calculate" as found in ancient Greek. It means to cast a vote or decide, not the use of a calculator or gematria. Believers can determine what the number means.

> Polybius, Plutarch, Palaeph., Anthol.; commonly and indeed chiefly in the middle in the Greek writings to give one's vote by casting a pebble into the urn; to decide by voting.
>
> – Thayer's Greek Lexicon

Another important term is that the Mark of the Beast can be counted as mankind – it is the total number of unbelievers on earth according to the Greek. Instead of rendering the Greek to English as "a man," it can be translated as simply "man." This means that the passage does not necessarily refer to a person like the antichrist.

The final crucial term is the number. It correlates to mankind, not the antichrist.

## What Does 666 Mean?

The number of the beast relates to its image. 666 is a distinct symbol of the beast and the people that compose its image. The role of the False Prophet is to attract others, whereby the replication of the beast's image into more and more followers advances that goal.

666 is the total symbolic number of people who decide to rebel against God and follow the beast as the image of its rebellious nature. Using force by wars or threats to be part of the beast is not as important as God letting people reject Him through their sin nature.

It boils down to free will in this case. Unbelievers will choose to make their own path to god or to be as god, while believers will reject free will and receive the gift of God's will.

The issue at hand is that for centuries the number of the beast has been associated with the antichrist. This forces the use of gematria or Bible codes in an attempt to derive any meaning. However, if the image of the beast is self-centered people, the mark of the beast is much easier for us to understand based upon letting the original Greek breathe freely.

We should look again at the three important terms to consider in verses 17 and 18 of Revelation chapter 13.

## Relationships of Keywords

**Man** – This means all unbelievers. Man can be plural for mankind.

**Calculate** – This means people who are righteous and who have understanding determine what the number of the beast means. This ties into Daniel 12:10 with the same concept that only the righteous will understand the Great Tribulation Period. If we are wise, we will let the Bible interpret itself. Revelation 13:18 states the number of the beast is the total number of unbelievers of humanity in our view.

**Number** – The total number of unbelievers is derived from the symbol of 666. This falls short of the symbol of 1000, which is a complete number (i.e., God owns the cattle on a thousand hills, meaning all cattle on all hills of the earth – see Psalm 50:10). Man will fall short of completion by trying to save himself during the last days of this age. Man was created on the 6th day, so mankind's association to the symbol of 6 is clear.

Finally, there is an interesting passage in Zechariah about two-thirds of the wicked being cut off. Perhaps it is a coincidence that two-thirds of 1000 is 666.

### Zechariah 13:7-9

*"Awake, O sword, against my shepherd,*
*against the man who stands next to me,"*
*declares the LORD of hosts.*
*"Strike the shepherd, and the sheep will be scattered;*
*I will turn my hand against the little ones.*
*In the whole land, declares the LORD,*
**two thirds shall be cut off and perish,**
*and one third shall be left alive.*

*And I will put this third into the fire,*
*and refine them as one refines silver,*
*and test them as gold is tested.*
*They will call upon my name,*
*and I will answer them.*
*I will say, 'They are my people';*
*and they will say, 'The LORD is my God.'"*

In the previous chapter, we proposed that the image of the beast is people, or in other words, a segment of society around us that will believe deceptive messages and put the lies into practice. Since we also know that the image causes the Mark, we see how the Mark of the Beast is increased in number as the false prophets gain more followers. It will not be just believing in the messages but acting on them like the symbol of the Mark on the right hand portrays. The hand is a symbol for action, so it does not mean every unbeliever is getting a chip implanted to buy or sell.

The end of the age will be like the Days of Noah. The judgments mentioned in Genesis 6 are primarily about sin and active rebellion of mankind, not about fallen angels, a famous figure or any other focus topic like implanted chips. Christ's predictions in Matthew 24 speak of warnings for average people not to be led astray by false prophets. This is the core warning message.

People of the earth will do regular things in the last days like getting married or going on vacation. However, there will come a point when the majority follows the beast system of lies and controls, then sudden destruction will come like in Noah's day. This is the Day of the Lord that comes after the 6th seal is opened when the worship of demons (known in the Bible as idols – Revelation 9:20-21) is prevalent during the wrath period of the bowls and trumpets.

There are many warnings in Revelation not to take the Mark. Here is one final warning:

Revelation 14:9-11 *And another angel, a third, followed them, saying with a loud voice, "If anyone worships the beast and its image and receives a mark on his forehead or on his hand, he also will drink the wine of God's wrath, poured full strength into the cup of his anger, and he will be tormented with fire and sulfur in the presence of the holy angels and in the presence of the Lamb. And the smoke of their torment goes up forever and ever, and they have no rest, day or night, these worshipers of the beast and its image, and whoever receives the mark of its name."*

# Chapter 32

## *Where Does Armageddon Take Place?*

### Where is Armageddon?

The age we live in closes out as Christ comes to earth and defeats those opposed to Him. They symbolically gather at the location named Armageddon. Is this an actual location like being centered around Jerusalem, or is this place a spiritual term for the entire earth at war with Christ and His followers?

> Revelation 16:12-16 *The sixth angel poured out his bowl on the great river Euphrates, and its water was dried up, to prepare the way for the kings from the east. And I saw, coming out of the mouth of the dragon and out of the mouth of the beast and out of the mouth of the false prophet, three unclean spirits like frogs. For they are demonic spirits, performing signs, who go abroad to the kings of the whole world, to assemble them for battle on the great day of God the Almighty. ("Behold, I am coming like a thief! Blessed is the one who stays awake, keeping his garments on, that he may not go about naked and be seen exposed!"). And they assembled them at the place that in Hebrew is called Armageddon.*

While it might be natural to wonder which city or country will host this physical event, Christ's return will be global and transcend national boundaries. Certainly, Jerusalem and surrounding areas will be involved, yet we know the entire earth will see Him as optic root words are used to describe His physical revelation. We previously studied that the same words used to describe the first advent of "God in the flesh" are also to describe His return in physical form. It will be a literal, visual second advent across the globe (Revelation 1:7).

We can go back to Old Testament passages to learn about more details that are described in Revelation, since it is mostly a book of repeated prophecies. The symbolic battle of Armageddon is connected to the end of the Day of the Lord period when Christ arrives on earth in His resurrected body. Isaiah 2 is an important Day of the Lord passage that gives us context.

Isaiah 2:9-11

*So man is humbled,*
*and each one is brought low—*
*do not forgive them!*
*Enter into the rock*
*and hide in the dust*
*from before the terror of the LORD,*
*and from the splendor of his majesty.*
*The haughty looks of man shall be brought low,*
*and the lofty pride of men shall be humbled,*
*and the LORD alone will be exalted in that day.*

The "hiding in rocks" concept is found in the 6th seal of Revelation 6:15. However, there will be no place to hide and there will be no army that can muster any threat against the coming of Christ as described in Joel 3.

Joel 3:9-16

*Proclaim this among the nations:*
*Consecrate for war;*
*stir up the mighty men.*

Let all the men of war draw near;
let them come up.
Beat your plowshares into swords,
and your pruning hooks into spears;
let the weak say, "I am a warrior."
Hasten and come,
all you surrounding nations,
and gather yourselves there.
Bring down your warriors, O LORD.
Let the nations stir themselves up
and come up to the Valley of Jehoshaphat;
for there I will sit to judge
all the surrounding nations.
Put in the sickle,
for the harvest is ripe.
Go in, tread,
for the winepress is full.
The vats overflow,
for their evil is great.
Multitudes, multitudes,
in the valley of decision!
For the day of the LORD is near
in the valley of decision.

The sun and the moon are darkened,
and the stars withdraw their shining.
The LORD roars from Zion,

*and utters his voice from Jerusalem,*
*and the heavens and the earth quake.*
*But the LORD is a refuge to his people,*
*a stronghold to the people of Israel.*

Joel 3 clearly points to the events of Revelation 6, 14, 16, and 19. There is a beginning period of Armageddon with a gathering, then an incredibly swift battle. The time between the gathering and the end of the battle is not known, yet the text does not portray a long period.

## Summary of Joel 3 Compared to Revelation

Revelation 16:16 and Revelation 19:19 point to the assembly of nations at odds with God as we notice in Joel 3:9-12.

Revelation 14:14-20 and 19:15 show the winepress analogy of Joel 3:13.

The Day of the Lord is referenced in Joel 3:15-16 and in Revelation 6:12.

Armageddon is not much of a battle. Christ speaks then the wicked fall. See these related passages – Isaiah 26:21; Daniel 7:11; 2 Thessalonians 1:7-8; 2 Thessalonians 2:8; Jude 1:14-15; Revelation 17:14; Revelation 19:15.

One fascinating concept within the meaning of Armageddon is the Valley of Decision found in Joel 3:14. This is a bottleneck where the earth will be divided between believers and unbelievers. There are also references to the location of Jehoshaphat's meeting in a background passage from 1 Kings 2 that describes a dividing line. We have all heard of the phrase "draw a line in the sand." It is interesting that God will separate the nations.

> Joel 3:2 *I will gather all the nations and bring them down to the Valley of Jehoshaphat. And I will enter into judgment with them there, on behalf of my people and my heritage Israel, because they have scattered them among the nations and have divided up my land,*

> Zechariah 14:3-5 *Then the LORD will go out and fight against those nations as when he fights on a day of battle. On that day his feet shall stand on the Mount of Olives that lies before Jerusalem on the east, and the Mount of Olives shall be split in two from east to west by a very wide valley, so that one half of the Mount shall move northward, and the other half southward. And you shall flee to the valley of my mountains, for the valley of the mountains shall reach to Azal. And you shall flee as you fled from the earthquake in the days of Uzziah king of Judah. Then the LORD my God will come, and all the holy ones with him.*

Valleys are symbols of separation. There will come a narrowing point when people side with God or the devil. This is the greatest test of humankind. Which side are you on? What if a family member was on the other side? What if being on the right side costs you your job or your house or your children?

> Luke 17: 30-37 *"so will it be on the day when the Son of Man is revealed. On that day, let the one who is on the housetop, with his goods in the house, not come down to take them away, and likewise let the one who is in the field not turn back. Remember Lot's wife. Whoever seeks to preserve his life will lose it, but whoever loses his life will keep it. I tell you, in that night there will be two in one bed. One will be taken and the other left. There will be two women grinding together. One will be taken and the other left." And they said to him, "Where, Lord?" He said to them, "Where the corpse is, there the vultures will gather."*

There is no need to find the location of Armageddon on a map. It is a bigger concept than that. People will use free will to rebel against God, but it is not really a choice, is it? It is human nature to fight God (see Free Will vs. Predestination and Predetermination article on Academia.edu).

> *Deuteronomy 30:19-20 I call heaven and earth to witness against you today, that I have set before you life and death, blessing and curse. Therefore choose life, that you and your offspring may live, loving the LORD your God, obeying his voice and holding fast to him, for he is your life and length of days, that you may dwell in the land that the LORD swore to your fathers, to Abraham, to Isaac, and to Jacob, to give them.*

Only Divine nature as the gift of the Holy Spirit saves us, keeps us as a guarantee of Christ's physical salvation, and to obtain the inheritance of eternal life in the fullness of time.

*Ephesians 1:7-14 In him we have redemption through his blood, the forgiveness of our trespasses, according to the riches of his grace, which he lavished upon us, in all wisdom and insight making known to us the mystery of his will, according to his purpose, which he set forth in Christ as **a plan for the fullness of time**, to unite all things in him, things in heaven and things on earth.*

*In him **we have obtained an inheritance, having been predestined** according to the purpose of him who works all things according to the counsel of his will, so that we who were the first to hope in Christ might be to the praise of his glory. In him you also, when you heard the word of truth, the gospel of your salvation, and believed in him, were **sealed with the promised***

***Holy Spirit, who is the guarantee of our inheritance until we acquire possession of it**, to the praise of his glory.*

We close with Christ's short explanation of the end of this age and the beginning of His age to come. It is important to consider the similarity between this passage and Luke 17's warning that people and families will be divided. We can see this division today, only to be intensified in the coming days. Thank God there is hope provided to keep us through these increasingly dark times by the protection of the Holy Spirit and the promise of rewards to come.

> Matthew 19:28-29 *Jesus said to them, "Truly, I say to you, in the new world, when the Son of Man will sit on his glorious throne, you who have followed me will also sit on twelve thrones, judging the twelve tribes of Israel.* ***And everyone who has left houses or brothers or sisters or father or mother or children or lands, for my name's sake****, will receive a hundredfold and will inherit eternal life."*

# Chapter 33

*When Are the 70 Weeks of Daniel?*

## Background Texts of the Great Tribulation Period

This is a bonus chapter for those who like to dig deeper into topics like Daniel's 70 weeks or the Abomination of Desolation. The basics have already been covered in previous chapters, so there is no need to continue if these topics are giving you a headache. Many people have tried to figure out some of the most difficult passages in the Bible like Daniel 9 and Daniel 11. This is a modest attempt.

The 3.5 year Great Tribulation Period begins at the mid-point of Daniel's 70th week prophecy in Daniel 9. We will coordinate with Daniel 2, 7 and 12 to understand this before getting deeper into the more difficult chapters.

The first 69 weeks of this prophecy were fulfilled in the past, so we will focus on what remains of Daniel's 70th week. A week, according to this prophecy, equals 7 years. The prophecy is stated in <u>Daniel 9:26-27</u> after the already fulfilled 69 weeks.

It is easiest to start with Daniel 2:40-45 as it provides the general outline of the beast that the final antichrist comes out of before correlation with Daniel 9.

> "And there shall be a fourth kingdom, strong as iron, because iron breaks to pieces and shatters all things. And like iron that crushes, it shall break and crush all these. And as you saw the feet and toes, partly of potter's clay and partly of iron, it shall be a divided kingdom, but some of the firmness of iron shall be in it, just as you saw iron mixed with the soft clay. And as the toes of the feet were partly iron and partly clay, so the kingdom shall be partly strong and partly brittle. As you saw the iron mixed with soft clay, so they will mix with one another in marriage, but they will not hold together, just as iron does not mix with clay. And **in the days of those kings the God of heaven will set up a kingdom** that shall never be destroyed, nor shall the kingdom be left to another people. **It shall break in pieces all these kingdoms and bring them to an end,** and it shall stand forever, just as you saw that a stone was cut from a mountain by no human hand, and that it broke in pieces the iron, the bronze, the clay, the silver, and the gold. A great God has made known to the king what shall be after this. The dream is certain, and its interpretation sure."

A close reading of this crucial passage reveals that these kings are part of the final beast (world empire), which is symbolically divided into ten kingdoms, as shown in Daniel 7:20-24 and Revelation 13:1, 17:12. The key statement is that God destroys the 10 kings / kingdoms at the end of time (not at 70 AD or 135 AD or throughout any of the times of the Gentiles). This happens when Christ comes at the second advent and destroys the final beast with the global 10 kingdoms.

## The Transition Period at the End of the Age

Daniel 2:40-43 = Daniel 7:20 = Daniel 7:24 = Revelation 13:1 = Revelation 17:12

Times of the Gentiles ending > Final beast of global kingdoms = 70th week

Jeremiah 30:11 prophesies that God will make an end of all nations (but leave Israel as the sole nation left on earth). Daniel 2 and Jeremiah 30 fit perfectly with Daniel 7:12 and the Revelation 20 reign period.

This begs a big question that should be at the top of our minds. Why would Christ come to destroy a global kingdom if He could just destroy the entire earth with everything in it? The answer is to establish His kingdom on earth, as we already know from previous studies. We also see survivors of the nations mentioned in Daniel 7:12, so the entire earth is not destroyed, since it will be cleansed.

The other key statement from Daniel 2 is the term "mountain," where a stone was cut out of it by no human hands. This is a metaphor of true Zion (and similar terms) of the future kingdom to be established on earth (Micah 4:1). Only God can establish this, as humanity has been inept at setting up a peaceful government.

Nobody on earth can make a Holy Place, destroy the beast, or do anything of true significance, because only God grants peace on earth with His desired worship system at a place He designates. Any attempts to build a Holy Place by human hands is not the true temple or city in the future age. We know He builds the city mentioned in Hebrews 11:16. Christ went to "prepare a place" for us that comes to be established on earth (Revelation 21:2-3). God also explains the plan in a vision to David through Nathan. A purely human son of David could not fulfill this prophecy.

*1 Chronicles 17:9-12 And I [God] will appoint a place for my people Israel and will plant them, that they may dwell in their own place and be disturbed no more. And violent men shall waste them no more, as formerly, from the time that I appointed judges over my people Israel. And I will subdue all your enemies. Moreover, I declare to you that the LORD will build you a house. When your days are fulfilled to walk with your fathers, I will raise up your offspring after you, one of your own sons, and I will establish his kingdom. He shall build a house for me, and I will establish his throne forever.*

Isaiah, Jeremiah, Ezekiel and other prophets all have remaining prophecies yet unfulfilled that are repeated in Revelation. Daniel, however, holds a unique position of stating time periods of identical lengths in the middle of the book of Revelation.

Times, time and half a time, 42 months and 1260 days all equal approximately 3.5 years. These times are the length of the Great Tribulation Period. It seems God does not want to consider the lengths as symbolic, since they are restated differently but yield the same result.

The time periods mentioned by Daniel are crucial to understand. Certainly, there has been tribulation since John wrote the prophecies, but the Great Tribulation Period occurs just before Christ comes back to earth. Daniel 7 is the most important chapter for timing and details that correlate to Revelation, since so much of Daniel's vision is repeated by John.

The end of the Great Tribulation period is easy to know because of the major marker of Christ destroying the final beast and final antichrist at His return (Revelation 19:19-20 compared to Daniel 7:11-26 and 2 Thessalonians 2:1-9).

## The End of the Age When the Antichrist is Destroyed

Daniel 7:11, 22, 26 = 2 Thessalonians 2:8 = Revelation 19:19-20

How can we know to figure out other markers without clear relationships? There are some who believe we are not supposed to know the timing of the end, yet there are passages to guide us and provide us with great warnings.

## The Thief in the Night

The sometimes vague and often confusing nature of these scriptural passages pose a significant problem in setting dates, since we were not given enough information to set them. There is a general sense that we are supposed to know a basic outline. Once these events take place, we can worry about date debates. The Church cannot know the timing today and could not know the "times or the seasons" in the past, as Christ stated to the apostles in Acts 1:7, but it is a different story when the season comes with signs.

We need to be awake, not in darkness, keep oil in the lamps, watch for signs, and remain ever vigilant. The purpose of signs is to watch out for them. Otherwise, we would not need signs if there was a concept of imminence promoted to be a surprise to believers. Christ could have simply stated that He will come back unexpectedly. He didn't say that or anything similar, because He will only come as a thief to those unprepared.

We already discussed in Chapter 1 that "no man knows (perceives) the day or the hour" doesn't mean what pre-trib rapture believers think it means today. We will absolutely know the general time and the season of Christ's coming. We will not "perceive" the day until the signs occur. This will be when the information is unveiled, with many signs established for the wise to understand the beginning of the end. We were given dire warnings to be prepared as we see events unfold.

There is certainly going to be a lot of false information along with false signs and wonders, so it is doubtful that many will believe in the true markers. We still need to keep our core focus to spread the message of the coming kingdom to earth as the completion of the gospel message while watching out for true signs. Being prepared may mean going into captivity or dying for Christ. Revelation provides us with statements for preparation.

There are three possible outcomes mentioned in the Bible for the saints during the Great Tribulation Period. We already discussed that God will not kill believers, because we are not destined for His wrath.

## End-time Options for the Saints

- **Martyrdom** – the beast government will have believers killed.
- **Captivity** – believers will "be in prison" – not able to buy or sell.
- **Preservation** – the elect will be carried on "eagles wings" or sealed.

# The Final Exodus

> Revelation 12:6 *"and the woman fled into the wilderness, where she has a place prepared by God, in which she is to be nourished for 1,260 days."*

We see plagues and the wilderness mentioned in Revelation. This correlates to the Exodus of God's people coming out of bondage. After

Christ ascended into Heaven in <u>Revelation 12:5</u>, we know Judea (a little later called Palestine) was completely taken over by the Romans. The Jews either died fighting the Romans or left. The early Church left. They were not in the fight and knew the <u>Luke 21</u> prophecy to flee Judea.

> <u>Revelation 12:1-6</u> *And a great sign appeared in heaven: a woman clothed with the sun, with the moon under her feet, and on her head a crown of twelve stars. She was pregnant and was crying out in birth pains and the agony of giving birth. And another sign appeared in heaven: behold, a great red dragon... And the dragon stood before the woman who was about to give birth, so that when she bore her child he might devour it. She gave birth to a male child, one who is to rule all the nations with a rod of iron, but her child was caught up to God and to his throne, and the woman fled into the wilderness, where she has a place prepared by God, in which she is to be nourished for 1,260 days.*

Notice the term 1,260 days—is it a symbol for the times of the Gentiles or Church age or something else, like Israel being scattered throughout the nations? Let's assume it simply means 1,260 literal days, since it matches the 3.5 year period of Daniel.

We will first examine the role of the Woman (Israel), who fled into the wilderness after Christ ascended to Heaven. The text does not say when she fled, but it is after the ascension. There could be a 2,000 year gap half way through verse 6 of Revelation 12. This verse after the ascension states that the Woman is to be nourished for 1,260 days, which is the same length as the Great Tribulation Period if we use actual days. We know that Daniel Chapter 12 also reported the protection of Israel during the greatest time of distress ever known.

The vision does not report how long the Woman is in the wilderness after the ascension. The only statement about time is that she is nourishment for 1,260 days, so we do not need to associate the wilderness length being 1,260 days.

We should also consider that the Woman (Israel) has a crown of 12 stars. This sign is a reference to Joseph (the 12-star dream of Genesis 37:9). Joseph is the archetype of the first advent work of the Messiah since Revelation 12 speaks to this period. His brothers rejected Him and were jealous. David and Judah are related to the second advent work of the Messiah, who will be crowned King by the nation and reign on earth.

> Genesis 37:8-9 *"His (Joseph's) brothers said to him, 'Are you indeed to reign over us? Or are you indeed to rule over us?' So they hated him even more for his dreams and for his words.*
>
> *Then he dreamed another dream and told it to his brothers and said, 'Behold, I have dreamed another dream. Behold, the sun, the moon, and eleven stars were bowing down to me.'"*

The vision of <u>Revelation 12:1</u> references this dream. Since the remaining nation of Israel rejected the Messiah at the first advent, there remains the need to fulfill prophecies. One is <u>Zechariah 12:10</u> that is repeated in <u>Revelation 1:7</u>. Israel needs to mourn and repent before they can accept the true Messiah. Unfortunately, however necessary, God needs to get their attention through the Great Tribulation Period.

Despite rising adversity and global calamity, God has prepared a place for Israel to be nourished in the Great Tribulation Period. This is like the Exodus example of a nation being kept alive in adverse conditions. Manna and water were provided during the first wilderness foreshadow. See <u>Exodus 19:4</u> and <u>Deuteronomy 1:30-33</u>, <u>32:10-14</u> examples.

One thing we know for sure is that God has scattered the Jews throughout the world. Based on textual evidence, we cannot definitively say that God is nourishing Israel or the Church in the wilderness during the time of the Gentiles. If the Congregation was to be protected for an extended length of time, there most likely would have been a different time symbol used that does not fit the 3.5 year period.

Scattering through the nations means dispersion of people. Wilderness is a place of preservation, so we should not confuse these terms. Wilderness timing does not mean diaspora. We get more answers in the following verses. The Woman is sent to the wilderness **after** Satan is cast out of Heaven, which is the same period as when the restrainer (Michael) steps aside.

Revelation 12:12 *"Therefore, rejoice, O heavens and you who dwell in them! But woe to you, O earth and sea, for the devil has come down to you in great wrath, because* **he knows that his time is short!'**

*13 And* **when** *the dragon saw that he had been thrown down to the earth, he pursued the woman who had given birth to the male child. 14 But the woman was given the two wings of the great eagle so that she might fly from the serpent into the wilderness, to the place where she is to be nourished for a time, and times, and half a time. 15 The serpent poured water like a river out of his mouth after the woman, to sweep her away with a flood. 16 But the earth came to the help of the woman, and the earth opened its mouth and swallowed the river that the dragon had poured from his mouth. 17 Then the dragon became furious with the woman and went off to make war on the rest of her offspring, on those who keep the commandments of God and hold to the testimony of Jesus. And he stood on the sand of the sea."*

We see 1,260 days in verse 6, while verse 14 mentions a time, times and half of time. Both terms are used by Daniel. They equal 3.5 years.

1,260 days = time, times, half of time = 42 months = 3.5 years = GTP

Verse 12 states that Satan's time is short. This is the authority given to him during the Great Tribulation Period. A short period fits best. If 1,260 days means 1,260 years or 2,000 years, we have an immediate conflict with this text conveying a short time period.

Verse 14 is the same wording as Daniel 7:25 and 12:7 timing. Revelation 12:6 = 12:14.

The end of Revelation 12 is a more detailed version of verse 6, but they are speaking about the same period after Satan is cast out of Heaven (when the restrainer Michael stands up).

Verses 14 to 16 associate the Woman as the one being preserved in the wilderness, but then verse 17 differentiates a separate offspring associated with the Woman. This makes sense with all Scripture as some passages state that satan will war against the saints and other passages state Israel will be preserved. It is possible that the Woman preserved is the 144,000 of Revelation 7:4, while the Church is differentiated in verse 17 since satan will be allowed to conquer the other offspring of the Woman.

In Hosea 2:14-16 we see the reason for the wilderness because God will lure His people back to Him in the end. Tribulation will occur (Deuteronomy 4:30), but God will not abandon His chosen people. Hosea alludes to the parallel of Exodus and the wilderness when Israel again states they will follow the true God in the future.

*"Therefore, behold, **I will allure her**, and bring her into the wilderness, and speak tenderly to her. And there I will give her her vineyards and make the Valley of Achor a door of hope.*

*And there she shall answer as in the days of her youth, as at the time when she came out of the land of Egypt.*

*And in that day, declares the LORD,*

*you will call me 'My Husband,'*

*and no longer will you call me 'My Baal.'"*

The mention of firstfruits in Revelation 14:4 gives us an answer of how to tie all of this together. The wilderness, the 144,000 and the correlation to Exodus are related to a most important aspect of the book of Revelation. The plagues, signs, and other events are to bring the *entire* nation of Israel back into the fold under Christ as one nation (not a separate Church or congregation from blood Israel).

Romans 11:25-26 *Lest you be wise in your own sight, I do not want you to be unaware of this mystery, brothers: a partial hardening has come upon Israel, until the fullness of the Gentiles has come in. And in this way all Israel will be saved, as it is written,*

*"The Deliverer will come from Zion, he will banish ungodliness from Jacob";*

Taken together, we can now see the way these major events coalesce into a coherent and organized method that takes the shape of God's plan. The Great Tribulation Period is when satan's spirit is loose to wreak havoc on the earth as he tries to go after the saints but the "earth" helps the Woman. The antichrist is allowed to conquer the saints temporarily, as shown in several passages. This dual salvation plan matches Revelation, since we can't have everyone being preserved or everyone being persecuted. There are clearly two groups mentioned in Revelation 12 (the Woman and her offspring). Both salvation plans occur simultaneously, itself a sign of the complexity and sophistication of the system taking shape during the end times.

## As in the Days of Noah

The analogies of Noah's flood and Sodom are used to describe the end times. Noah went through the flood but was spared wrath. Was it easy on Noah? No way! Noah actually went through the flood just as believers will go through great tribulation. See 2 Peter 2 for more information on judgment upon the earth.

Lot completely escaped destruction but lost his wife. This was tribulation for Lot. People will especially be tested in the end times. We need to trust God's word (look for answers found in Scripture, not trust ourselves). Everything we need to know today has already been provided to us. The two witnesses will shed some more light for the elect, but we have enough information now.

Matthew 24:36-43 *"But concerning that day and hour no one knows, not even the angels of heaven, nor the Son, but the Father only. For as were the days of Noah, so will be the coming of the Son of Man. For as in those days before the flood they were eating and drinking, marrying and giving in marriage, until the day when Noah entered the ark, and* **they** *were unaware until the flood came and swept them all away, so will be the coming of the Son of Man. Then two men will be in the field; one will be taken and one left. Two women will be grinding at the mill; one will be taken and one left. Therefore, stay awake, for* **you** *do not know on what day your Lord is coming. But know this, that if the master of the house had known in what part of the night the thief was coming, he would have stayed awake and would not have let his house be broken into."*

This passage is about two groups of people – "they" and "you." "**They**" are the unwise and won't be saved. "**You**" are believers who are to keep oil in the lamps, be prepared, and keep watch. See 1 Thessalonians 5:1-10 and Revelation 16:15.

The most important aspect of being prepared is to be righteous as we see Christ speaking to the Church of Sardis in Revelation 3:1b-5.

*"I know your works. You have the reputation of being alive, but you are dead. Wake up, and strengthen what remains and is about to die, for I have not found your works complete in the sight of my God. Remember, then, what you received and heard. Keep it, and repent. If you will not wake up, I will come like a thief, and you will not know at what hour I will come against you. Yet you have still a few names in Sardis, people who have not soiled their garments, and they will walk with me in white, for they are worthy. The one who conquers will be clothed thus in white garments, and I will never blot his name out of the book of life. I will confess his name before my Father and before his angels."*

We see in <u>1 Thessalonians 5:1-10</u> and in Christ's message to Sardis that it is the unrighteous who will be overtaken, like the thief analogy where the righteous will not be surprised or unprepared. Righteousness is the main message. The Church needed to be prepared for 2000 years, so a surprise rapture changes nothing of this core message to always be righteous.

A pre-trib rapture would be a clear sign of missing people on earth and a different message to unbelievers. God does not state this anywhere. It goes against false signs and wonders to get people to consider the false god. God is fairly placing the world in the greatest test ever, so there is no exemption from this. It would be a detriment to His plan if the Church is missing.

The main message in the middle of this book of Revelation is that God will allow the test of the entire world to take the Mark of the Beast. We also see specific groups of people to be tested – blood Israel and the Church in the Great Tribulation.

## Daniel's 70th Week

Daniel 12:7 = Revelation 11:2 = Revelation 12:14 – we see a 3.5 year period for key events of the nation of Israel at the end of this age, which was part of Daniel's original prophecy relating to the city and Holy Place in Daniel 9:24. We need to remember that the Book of Revelation up to Chapter 19 completes the 70 week prophecy of Daniel, so we always should keep the 70th week in reference as to the goals stated in Daniel 9:24. It is about cleansing the Holy People, the city and Holy Place. Christ did all the work to cleanse the people, but the Holy Place needs to be cleansed before the New Jerusalem can be established (Revelation 21:2). The bride of Christ is not ready (Revelation 19:7).

### The Mid-Point of Daniel's 70th Week

Daniel 7:25 = Revelation 13:5 – the final beast system with the antichrist has 3.5 years of power. This is the halfway point of Daniel's 70th week of Daniel 9:27.

The key timing in the 70th week is the covenant for 7 years (1 week) and the break in the mid-week. This time period agrees with a 3.5 year period. The prophecy is stated in Daniel 9:26-27 after the already fulfilled 69 weeks. Here are the important statements of this passage relating to the 70th week:

*"the people of **the prince** who is to come shall destroy the city and the sanctuary"*
*"And **he** shall make a strong covenant with many for one week"*
*"for half of the week **he** shall put an end to sacrifice and offering"*
*"on the wing of abominations shall come **one** who makes desolate"*
*"until the decreed end is poured out on the **desolator**"*

Some have jumped to the conclusion that Christ is the person confirming the covenant mentioned by Daniel 9 as establishing the new covenant, along with many other theories on Daniel's 70 weeks. However, Daniel 9:26 states that the prince of the people (who destroyed the second temple) will make this covenant, so the prince in verse 26 is not speaking of Christ. Previous statements in Daniel 9:25 speak of a completely different prince and earlier in verse 26 it speaks to an anointed one (which many believe to be Christ).

Prince and anointed one are not associated together in verse 26. Verse 26 shifts to the second temple destruction in AD 70 but ties in the "people" who destroyed it with a future "prince" (not the previously mentioned "anointed one" as he is "cut off" and "has nothing" according to <u>Daniel 9:26a</u>).

The prince of Daniel 9:27 is from the "people" of the final beast empire (mentioned in Daniel chapters 2 and 7). We previously studied the transition of the 4th and 5th kingdoms of these chapters in Daniel. Rome's system spread throughout the earth and will form the final beast empire, even though Rome itself does not resurrect.

This prince is the antichrist (called the "little horn" or the man of sin that Paul called the "man of lawlessness"). This verse is the key verse to Daniel's 70th week. It describes a covenant and sacrifices that we need to understand.

*"Seventy weeks are decreed about your people and your holy city"* – total time needed.

*"to finish the transgression, to put an end to sin"* – not fulfilled.

*"and to atone for iniquity"* – fulfilled by Christ.

*"to bring in everlasting righteousness"* – this will be fulfilled in the new earth that is prophesied in 2 Peter 3:13 and other new earth passages.

*"to seal both vision and prophet"* – John the Baptist was the last prophet to date, but another prophet will come as at least one of the 2 witnesses will be a prophet.

*"and to anoint a most holy place."* – this is the key part of the verse that we have been looking for. Is it a temple or where the New Jerusalem will reside? The latter makes the most sense, as we know the throne of God will come to dwell with His people (Revelation 21:2-3).

Daniel 9:24 outlines what will be accomplished during the 70 weeks. Verses 25-27 explain an overview of the entire 70 weeks.

Daniel 9:25-27 *"Know therefore and understand that from the going out of the word to restore and build Jerusalem to the coming of an anointed one, a prince, there shall be seven weeks. Then for sixty-two weeks it shall be built again with squares and moat, but in a troubled time. And after the sixty-two weeks, an anointed one shall be cut off and shall have nothing. And the people of the prince who is to come shall destroy the city and the sanctuary. Its end shall come with a flood, and to the end there shall be war. Desolations are decreed. And he shall make a strong covenant with many for one week, and for half of the week he shall put an end to sacrifice and offering. And on the wing of abominations shall come one who makes desolate, until the decreed end is poured out on the desolator."*

**Verse 25a** – an anointed one by God is Cyrus (Isaiah 45:1), who made the decree to rebuild the temple at first but was also prophesied to allow rebuilding of Jerusalem in Isaiah 44:26-28. The city is a key focus for the 70 weeks, not any temple since only the Holy Place is referenced (God will be the temple in the future). See Revelation 21:22.

7 weeks pass (49 years for a standard calendar or 50 years when using a Jubilee calendar) from the decree to the coming anointed prince. Cyrus may not be the anointed prince in verse 25, but he is

certainly associated with God's decree and original anointing. "Prince" can also mean leader, and we see a few options from the Bible – Zerubbabel, Artaxerxes, and Nehemiah.

Zerubbabel – see Zechariah 4:6 and 4:14 for the Spirit's anointing to use him. Joshua the Priest was also anointed with Zerubbabel but a priest is not mentioned in Daniel's prophecy. The focus is about the city, not the temple. This period is too early because Zerubbabel is not 49 or 50 years apart from Cyrus.

Nehemiah may be a better option for timing, yet he is not stated specifically to be anointed – see Nehemiah 5:14 where he is appointed. Nehemiah is appointed under Artaxerxes.

In Ezra 6:14 Cyrus, Darius, and Artaxerxes are all connected under the same decree originally prophesied by Isaiah. However, we do not need to worry about who the first anointed leader is. This has been fulfilled. The Isaiah > Cyrus > decree fulfilled by Artaxerxes may be the best fulfillment, but it is water under the bridge now.

**Gap** – there is a clear separation of 7 weeks from the 62 weeks. Why not just state 69 weeks? It is because there was a time gap in rebuilding the city (the city project was on hold for many years from Cyrus' decree until released again by Artaxerxes). The temple was built first under Zerubbabel, then the wall by Nehemiah, so that finally the city could be rebuilt after fortification.

There was the 70 literal year prophecy of Jeremiah that ended with a small initial return from exile under Zerubbabel and Joshua but the rebuilding of the city did not begin until later, after its wall was complete in Nehemiah 6:15. People returning and building a temple do not coincide with the rebuilding of the entire city. The city could not be rebuilt until the wall was complete, because Nehemiah only built a few houses besides the wall. The wall may have been built around 444 BC, but the timing is not clear. There are many discrepancies between Persian, Jewish, and Greek calendars.

**Verse 25b** – the city is built during the 62 weeks (after the 7 week period and time gap of being on hold). This 62 week period brings the timing to Herod's upgrade of the city and the temple. The total is 434 years using a standard calendar or 443 years when using a Jubilee calendar. It is not clear when the 62 week prophecy finished. The Jews stated it took 46 years to complete Herod's second temple upgrade to Zerubbabel's temple (John 2:20). This was ~ 26-30 AD.

The textual data never definitively declares whether the city was rebuilt after 444 BC and finished before 30 AD, but let's not let that cloud our understanding of what can be securely gathered concerning the end times. The next verse is laser focused on the end. We simply need to realize that the 69 weeks are complete and that the law of atonement sacrifices were made invalid after the time of Christ, so this closed out the 69 weeks. Then the times of the Gentiles began as Christ prophesied and Paul stated in Romans 11:25-27.

**Verse 26a** – a different anointed one is mentioned, who is cut off after the 62 week rebuilding of the city period. John the Baptist and Christ are the best options of anointed ones (both were cut off during this time period). There is no mention of a prince (or leader) in verse 26a. Priests and prophets can be anointed just like kings or princes.

It is most likely that Christ is the anointed one in verse 26a since Daniel 9:24 states one of the 70 week prophecies is to atone for iniquity and Christ fulfilled this. After the 62 week period, the anointed one is "cut off" like Zechariah 13:8-9 where a large portion of Israel is cut off (as meaning perished in this passage).

The anointed one also "has nothing." This could mean Christ did not fulfill the kingly anointing during His first advent. He was anointed as the Messiah (as the Priest), yet did not receive the rights of King of Jerusalem at that time. The Jews rejected him. He is King of Kings in Heaven but not yet the King ruling over Jerusalem on earth. Christ was not anointed as King by the Jews.

The verse then shifts to the next phase of the prophecy.

## The Second Temple's Destruction and Transition to the 70th Week

**Verse 26b** – the prince is the antichrist and is not stated as being anointed or to live during the Second Temple period.

**Verse 26b** – the people to come are the Romans (morphed into the final beast of Daniel and Revelation).

**Verse 27** – "he" who makes the covenant is the prince of 26b (the antichrist).

The covenant made by the antichrist is over a 7 year period but does not necessarily need to be a 7 year covenant. It simply lasts for 7 years. It can be a permanent covenant that is void in 7 years when Christ comes. The covenant changes in 3.5 years. This is when the antichrist reveals his cards.

This all leads us to believe that it is not a covenant only about sacrifices. The first 3.5 years will be favorable to the Jews who are looking for the Messiah and rebuilding a temple, while the last 3.5 years will reveal the true intent of the covenant made with "many." Who is "many"? Who is the covenant made with? It is not the Mosaic covenant or new covenant because the terms will change when the abomination occurs. The sacrifices cease when the Abomination of Desolation occurs "on the wing of abomination." This event causes the sacrifices to cease. This is when the antichrist is revealed, as stated by Paul. The antichrist is also called the "desolator" in Daniel 9:27.

It is not clear if the antichrist tries to enforce a previous covenant or makes a new covenant. The covenant is most likely first about land to enable a sacrificial system and other worship systems. The outer court was stated as given to the nations (Gentiles) in Revelation 11:2. We need to consider that since the antichrist is non-Jewish that he can only allow the Jews to set up a sacrificial system. Most likely, this world government power will take over the Holy Place area and grant the Jews an allowance to set up a temple, or it may be a grant from Islamic leadership.

The covenant's primary goal is to gain control of the temple mount land, which lends credibility to the practices that would take place on it. Once the land covenant is established, the final beast government will open the door to allowing sacrifices to be made on this land controlled by the world government of 10 kingdoms at first, but the little horn who rises out of this group will put a stop to the sacrifices when he claims to be god. One plausible scenario is that it may start with a non-obvious looking agreement with the U.N. or Islamic nations parsing out the temple mount area to be controlled by Gentiles so other monotheistic sects can have more access to it (Revelation 11:2).

The beginning of the covenant probably allows the establishment of a sacrificial system in the temple mount area but does not need to state specific terms of sacrifices. Controlling the land where the sacrifices are to be made is the first step. The covenant will most likely provide an allowance for the Jews. There will be sacrifices made in Jerusalem 3.5 years into this covenant. At the end of 3.5 years, the antichrist will stop the sacrifices and claim to be god. Then the Great Tribulation Period begins.

2 Thessalonians 2:4 states the antichrist will abolish all worship systems, not just the temple mount system established. The entire world will be affected. We should realize this is not about the Jews only or the Church. It is about deceiving the masses on earth. Most certainly, there will be lies about the true God (the creator and sustainer of life). The false god will make claims, but the wise will understand they are not true. The unwise will believe the claims.

Spirits have manipulated kings throughout the ages (that God has allowed to happen, like everything else as part of His plan to eventually reunite Heaven and earth). Sometimes God uses kings directly (example of Cyrus in Isaiah 44:28 and 45:1-7) and sometimes God allows satan to control governments. Notice that God clearly allows calamity through other kings, like Isaiah 45:7 states that God created tribulation. Nobody likes to think about this, but we can simply say that God created satan.

Satan rebelled, yet God allows him to operate. He didn't utterly destroy satan when he rebelled. Proverbs 16:4 states that it is because of His purpose. God didn't create evil directly, but He created beings that disobeyed, so God allows evil indirectly as part of His plan. We can't ignore Isaiah 45:7 or Proverbs 16:4 just because we don't like to think about God allowing evil in the world. It was part of His plan to reunite Heaven and earth as He foreknew angels and people would rebel. His allowance of evil is great wisdom.

Even though we do not understand God's predetermination, we should notice the same concept of God allowing this false god to rise in the end times. It is for His purpose like shown in Ephesians 1:9-11 to unite everything in Heaven and on earth. We can surmise that it is because He wants more people to be tested, tried, and saved, so He allows evil to continue since the time of the fall of satan.

A lot of these topics will increase in clarity with the signs as days proceed until culmination. For now, we have enough knowledge. His grace is sufficient. His love abounds to all. His hope is close at hand.

Psalm 22:19

*But you, O LORD, do not be far off!*
*O you my help, come quickly to my aid!*

# Appendix 1

## *Outline of Interpretive Methodology*

This summary explains an objectively orientated interpretation of the Bible.

Subjectivity (personal interpretation) is not capable of tailoring truth found in the Bible since it comes to us "As Is". See 1 Corinthians 2:11-16 and 2 Peter 1:20-21.

Truth is objective. It came from God to apostles & prophets by divine revelation.

Our free will or determination cannot extract truth from within since our hearts are depraved (Mark 7:21-23). His spirit comes from outside of us into our hearts so we can know truth. See Romans 8:5-9.

God does not change (Malachi 3:6). His truth never changes or needs to be adapted because it is perfect (James 1:17).

We should not make an interpretation fit our preconceived notions or cultural tendencies.

Whether a Bible passage contains literal or figurative language, there must be an objectively true meaning. For example, the "heart" is a figurative term, but it refers to the reality of our innermost being as we are connected to the spiritual realm (Romans 5:5).

Figurative language in the Bible often speaks of events that take place in the heavenly realm or spiritual realm, so they "literally" occur even though we need metaphors to describe the unseen.

There is a physical realm (seen) and a heavenly realm (unseen).

The two realms meet in the spirit realm. For example, we on earth have a relationship with our heavenly Father because His Spirit dwells within us (Ephesians 2:18-22).

This leaves us with six possibilities for interpretation of any passage:
1. Literal language speaking of the physical realm
2. Literal language speaking of the heavenly realm
3. Literal language speaking of dual-realm interaction (spirit realm)
4. Figurative language speaking of the physical realm
5. Figurative language speaking of the heavenly realm
6. Figurative language speaking of dual-realm interaction (spirit realm)

The realms interrelate in this fashion:

The Father resides in the heavenly realm where the Son is now located.

The Son was located in the earthly realm during His first advent.

The Spirit "proceeds" from the Father and the Son in a dual-realm interaction (where heaven and earth meet). See Galatians 4:6 for an example of all realms interacting.

Following his resurrection, the Son is at the "right hand" of the Father in the heavenly realm (Ephesians 1:20). He is the first dual-realm being, referred to in the Bible as the last Adam (1 Corinthians 15:45).

The earth and all believers will become part of this dual-realm merger after Christ's second coming. Ephesians 1:9-10 describes this event at the end of the age.

With this background from Ephesians, we can better understand God's truth through symbols like New Jerusalem coming to the restored earth (Revelation 21:1-2). The unseen will be seen at the merger of Heaven and earth.

This example shows how the Book of Revelation can be interpreted by other passages in the Bible. The Bible gives us faith to believe and understand through the work of the Holy Spirit (Galatians 3:2-6).

Another set of examples from the Old and New Testaments display repeated language that states God "pours out his Spirit." The same God that poured his Spirit upon the Old Testament saints reveals His truth to us through His word:

*"If you turn at my reproof, behold, **I will pour out my spirit** to you; **I will make my words known** to you." —*Proverbs 1:23

*"God's love has been **poured out into our hearts through the Holy Spirit**, who has been given to us." —*Romans 5:5

*"[God] has also put his seal on us and **put his Spirit in our hearts** as a guarantee." —*2 Corinthians 1:22

Joel 2:28 is repeated in Acts 2:17: *"And in the last days it shall be, God declares, that **I will pour out my Spirit on all flesh**."*

# Appendix 2

## *Verb Tenses of Salvation*

The following passages describe salvation timing based upon past or present tense spiritual salvation language, or utilize future tense salvation language describing the resurrection of the dead. Some passages describe both types of salvation – spiritual salvation and salvation through bodily resurrection.

**Present** Tense = current state of spiritual salvation

**Future** Tense = focus on salvation at the resurrection

**Both** Tenses = present and future salvation mentioned

**Mostly** = focus on one verb tense over another when both are stated

Job 19:25-27 – Future

Isaiah 26:19-21 – Future

Daniel 7:22 + 12:2 – Future

Matthew 24:30-31– Future

Matthew 25:31-34 – Future

John 3:1-18 – Present

John 5:24-29 – Mostly Future

John 6:39-40 – Both

Romans 8:16-24 – Mostly Future

1 Corinthians 4:5 – Future

1 Corinthians 15:12-28 – Future

2 Corinthians 5:1-10 – Future

2 Corinthians 6:1-2 – Present

1 Thessalonians 4:13-17 – Future

1 Thessalonians 5:1-9 – Future

2 Thessalonians 2:1-12 – Future

2 Timothy 1:9-12 – Mostly Present

2 Timothy 4:8 – Future

Ephesians 2:4-9 – Mostly Present

Philippians 3:10-21 – Future

Colossians 3:1-4 – Both

Titus 2:11-13 – Both

Hebrews 9:27-28 – Future

1 Peter 1:3-9 – Both

1 Peter 5:4 – Future

1 John 2:28-3:2 – Mostly Future

Jude 20-24 – Both

# Appendix 3

## The 7 Seals Explained by Matthew 24

| Seal # | Revelation | Matthew | Terms |
|--------|-----------|---------|-------|
| 1 | 6:2 | 24:5 | Conquer |
| 2 | 6:4 | 24:6-7 | War |
| 3 | 6:5-6 | 24:7 | Famine |
| 4 | 6:8 | 24:7-8 | Death |
| 5 | 6:9-10 | 24:9-13 | Martyrs |
| N/A | 14:6-7 | 24:14 | Gospel |
| N/A | 13:5-8 | 24:15-27 | Abomination |
| 6 | 6:12 | 24:29 | Sun & Moon |
| 6 | 6:13-14 | 24:29 | Sky Signs |
| 6 | 6:15-16 | 24:30 | Hiding |
| 6 | 6:17 | 24:30 | Wrath |
| 7 | 8:1 | 24:30-31 | 2nd Advent |
| 7 | 8:3-4 | | Prayers |
| 7 | 8:5 | | Finality |

# Appendix 4

## *Jude and 2 Peter in Relation to the O.T.*

| Terms | OT Passage | 2 Peter | Jude |
|---|---|---|---|
| False Prophets | Numbers 16:2-3 | 2:1 | 1:4 |
| Rebellion | Genesis 3:4-5 | 2:4 | 1:6 |
| Destruction | Zephaniah 3:8 | 2:6 | 1:7 |
| False Prophets | Ezekiel 13:9 | 2:10 | 1:8 |
| False Prophets | Numbers 22:22-35 | 2:11 | 1:9 |
| Sin Nature | Proverbs 16:4-5 | 2:12 | 1:10 |
| Divination | Joshua 13:22 | 2:15 | 1:11 |
| Deception | Jeremiah 7:8-10 | 2:13 | 1:12a |
| Eternal Judgment | Psalm 49:14 | 2:17 | 1:12b-13 |
| Judgment Day | Isaiah 13:9-13 | 2:9 | 1:15 |
| Boasting | Psalm 49:13 | 2:18 | 1:16 |
| Rebellion | Daniel 12:9-10 | 3:3 | 1:18 |

# Appendix 5

## Revelation 18 Compared to Isaiah and Ezekiel

| Terms | Revelation | Ezekiel | Isaiah |
|---|---|---|---|
| Sorcery-Divination | 18:2 | | 47:9-13 |
| Trade-Wealth | 18:3 | 27:33 | 47:5 |
| Arrogance | 18:7 | 27:3 | 47:8 |
| Swift Judgment | 18:8 | 27:27 | 47:9 |
| Loss of Wealth | 18:9 | 27:32 | |
| Swift Judgment | 18:10 | 27:27 | 47:9 |
| Trade-Wealth | 18:11-16 | 27:4-27 | 47:15 |
| Loss of Wealth | 18:18 | 27:32 | |
| Mourning Loss | 18:19 | 27:30-31 | |
| Sorcery-Divination | 18:21-23 | | 47:9-13 |
| Judgment | 19:1-3 | 28:18-19 | 47:3-4 |

# Appendix 6

## *Revelation 17 Compared to O.T. Passages*

| Term or Phrase | Revelation | References |
|---|---|---|
| Seated on Waters | 17:1 | Jer 51:13 |
| Immorality | 17:2 | Jer 51:7 |
| Aligned with Beast | 17:3 | Dan 7:7 |
| Abominations | 17:4 | Jer 51:7 |
| Babylon the Great | 17:5 | Nah 3:4 |
| Blood of Martyrs | 17:6 | Rev 6:9-10 |
| Seated on Waters | 17:15 | Jer 51:13 |
| Destruction | 17:16 | Jer 51:1 |
| Great City | 17:18 | Gen 10:8-12 |

# Appendix 7

## History of Satan Acting Through the Beast

| Location or Time | Body on Earth | Acting Through | Form of Influence | Beast Head |
|---|---|---|---|---|
| Eden | Yes | Serpent | Physical | Wounded |
| Babel | | Nimrod | Spiritual | 2nd |
| Egypt | | Pharaohs | Spiritual | 3rd |
| Mesopotamia | | Kings | Spiritual | 4th |
| Greece | Prototype | Kings | Spiritual | 5th |
| Rome | | Emperors | Spiritual | 6th |
| Nations | | Leaders | Spiritual | ↓ |
| 10 Kingdoms | | Beast | Spiritual | 7th |
| Tribulation | Yes | Antichrist | Physical | Healed |
| Prison | | | None | No |

- The devil has influenced many events on the earth through various leaders via the spiritual realm.

- Beast heads are symbolic to represent the devil's activity on earth, whether direct or indirect.

- The beast is not a separate being from the devil. It cannot operate by itself since it is an extension.

- The devil has authority on earth that is channeled through the beast (Revelation 13:1-2).

- The prophecy about the serpent stated in Genesis 3:14-15 is alluded to in Revelation 13:3.

- The devil has influenced many events on the earth through various leaders via the spiritual realm.

- Beast heads are symbolic to represent the devil's activity on earth, whether direct or indirect.

- The beast is not a separate being from the devil. It cannot operate by itself since it is an extension.

- The devil has authority on earth that is channeled through the beast (Revelation 13:1-2).

# Appendix 8

*Passages about the Antichrist*

| Terms | Daniel | 2 Thes | Rev |
|:---:|:---:|:---:|:---:|
| Emergence | 7:8 | 2:9 | 11:7 |
| Boasting | 7:11 | 2:4 | 13:5 |
| Globalism | 7:20 | | 17:12-13 |
| Wars | 7:21 | | 13:7 |
| Revealed | 7:24 | 2:3 | 13:1 |
| Authority | 7:25 | 2:9 | 13:7 |
| Abomination | 7:25 | 2:4 | 13:6 |
| 3.5 Years | 7:25 | | 13:5 |
| Lawless | 7:25 | 2:3 | |
| Judgment | 7:22 | | 17:11-14 |
| Destroyed | 7:26 | 2:8 | 19:20 |

# Appendix 9

## *Key Concepts About the False Prophets*

**Review** – look for connecting keywords and relationships in Revelation 13 using the numbering system (Worship=1, etc., as shown below)

1. **Worship** – people will follow(1) the beast after experiencing physical(4) and spiritual(5) influence. 1 comes after 4 and 5.
2. **Authority / Power Given** – false prophets are allowed(2) to have the authority(2) of the devil. 2 leads way to 3 then 4.
3. **Deception** – signs & marvels(3) will be displayed after authority(2) is granted. 3 comes after 2.
4. **Makes / Forces** – people need to be convinced by these deceptive(3) measures of power that will be exercised(4) before people will follow(1) the beast. 4 comes after 3, resulting in 1.
5. **Presence** – the image of the beast will spread through the spirit(5) realm to people. 5 leads to 1.

# Revelation 13 Key Verses and Terms –

Please find the relationships of the numbers in parentheses that match the terms from the numbering system above.

---

*the whole earth marveled(3) as they followed(1) the beast.*

---

*they worshiped(1) the dragon, for he had given(2) his authority(2) to the beast,*

---

*they worshiped(1) the beast, saying, "... Who can fight against it?"*

---

*it was allowed(2) to make war(4) on the saints and to conquer(4) them.*

---

*the beast was given(2) a mouth... it was allowed(2) to exercise(4)authority(2)* authority(2) was given it over every tribe and people and language and nation, all who dwell on earth will worship(1) it,

[The False Prophet] exercises(4) all the authority(2) of the first beast in its presence(5),

and makes(4) the earth and its inhabitants worship(1) the first beast

It performs great signs(3), even making fire come down from heaven(3) to earth

by the signs that it is allowed to work(2) in the presence(5) of the beast it deceives(3) those who dwell on earth, telling them to make(4) an image(5) for the beast

it was allowed(2) to give breath(5) to the image(5) of the beast, so that the image(5) of the beast might even speak and might *cause(4) those who would not worship(1) the image(5) of the beast to be slain.*

*it causes(4) all..., to be marked on the right hand or the forehead,*

*so that no one can buy or sell unless he has the mark.*

We hope you enjoyed this book and learned how Revelation will help us get through tough times ahead. Please feel free to contact the author if you have any questions – KJ@kjsoze.eom